DECENT EXPOSURE

DECENT EXPOSURE

HOW TO MANAGE YOUR OWN PUBLICITY

VINCENT YEARLEY

KOGAN
PAGE

First published in 1991

Kogan Page Limited
120 Pentonville Road
London N1 9JN

© Vincent Yearley 1991

British Library Cataloguing in Publication Data

A CIP record for this book is available from the British Library.

ISBN 0-7494-0107-9
ISBN 0-7494-0108-7 Pbk

Typeset by DP Photosetting, Aylesbury, Bucks
Printed and bound in Great Britain by
Biddles Ltd, Guildford and King's Lynn

Contents

Acknowledgements

I would like to thank The Reading Newspaper Company Ltd, publishers of the *Reading Chronicle*, and H Bauer Publishing, producers of *Bella* magazine, both of whom allowed me to quote material for analysis.

I am also grateful to Wall to Wall Television, producers of Channel 4's *The Media Show*, who provided a video tape with useful background for the chapter on crisis management, and John Francis, editor of the *Luton Citizen*, for his assistance with the chapter on pictures. My sister Ruth was very helpful with the market research section; she too merits a mention.

Special thanks to Diane and Joanna for their unending patience and encouragement. Without their support, this book would never have happened.

CHAPTER 1
Who Needs Publicity?

What is 'news'?

A journalist once told me: 'News – real, hard news – is something that somebody, somewhere, wants kept quiet.'

He had a point; a fair proportion of what appears in our newspapers falls into the category of exposé, or investigative journalism. Notable examples of this type of news are sharp practice among unscrupulous landlords and the horrendous side-effects of certain commercially available drugs. Both were rightly brought into the public domain through the diligence of investigative reporters and campaigning editors.

But a glance at any daily paper will tell you that the 'hard news' definition above falls well short of what *typically* fills our news pages. That's because many news stories – motorway accidents, earthquakes, train crashes etc – just happen, and need to be reported immediately. Add some political stories, a few features and (with the exception of the *Independent*) an insatiable demand for pictures of the Royal Family and you have the basis of a typical 'news' day.

But, more interesting to you, there is another important ingredient in the media cake. Many stories get into print (or on the air) simply because they are handed to journalists on a plate by people *actively seeking coverage*. In fact, there are so many different organisations and individuals craving favourable editorial treatment that the average journalist is actually bombarded with material, usually (but not always) from those in the public relations (PR) industry.

A busy news editor, always rushing to meet the next deadline, will throw most of it in the bin, muttering under his or her breath: 'If you want an advert, mate, buy a space.' That's because half-baked attempts to win 'puff' are almost certain to fail; no journalist is going to use material that is simply a thinly veiled advert dressed up as an editorial. In fact, wherever possible, the journalist will take a positive delight in rejecting such material.

Journalists tend to guard their independence from commercial pressures. And woe betide you if you have the arrogance to think that taking an ad in a publication *automatically* entitles you to a free plug in the editorial columns. (There are, however, certain exceptions – see Chapter 4, for example.)

Try this experiment: pick up your daily paper and look closely at the stories; not just the front page stuff, but the smaller items inside as well. Mentally make three columns: winners, losers and no-scores.

'Losers' will be the stories that somebody would prefer not to see in the paper, while 'no-scores' will be the stories which just 'happen' (ie, where the treatment given to the subject makes little difference to anybody). The 'winners', on the other hand, will be the favourable stories, the ones which are beneficial to an organisation or individual.

At the simplest level, *Decent Exposure* is aimed at making you a 'winning' organisation in the media game. It sets out not so much to show you the sort of news coverage that people want kept *out*, as the sort of coverage that people (like you and those in the 'winners' category) actually want to get *in*. To paraphrase my opening quote, the editorial material you will provide will be something that somebody, somewhere, will want to read.

But just a minute. Before we get embroiled in all the detail and techniques, let's ask ourselves a few objective questions.

Why do you want publicity?

First of all, what is the point of drumming up editorial coverage? More precisely, what does it actually *achieve*?

Will a favourable write-up in the *Sun*, Britain's biggest selling daily newspaper, make your fortune? Or does a mention on your local radio station mean that you will be flooded with all the business you will ever need? If you are seeking new volunteers for your charity, or students for your course, or a greater audience for your presentation, will you find them by getting a passing reference in your local newspaper?

To be honest, no, not really. It is extremely difficult to quantify the effect of successful editorial exposure, especially in the short term. One-off mentions are useful, but are unlikely to produce any significant quantifiable benefits for your organisation. To be fair, though, the same problem applies to individual adverts – and they cost you money!

But here perhaps is part of our answer: marketing professionals don't seriously expect results from one-off ads, but they do expect tangible benefits from a properly co-ordinated advertising campaign. Your PR campaign should be run on the same lines; see it as a valid long-term boost to your day-to-day business or activities rather than a 'magic wand', immediately solving all your problems.

Meanwhile, don't forget your hidden benefits. Every single message from you to any of your 'publics' is valid as a builder of confidence. In other words, although not immediately quantifiable, your PR efforts could make a significant difference when you and your potential customer/user do finally come into direct contact with each other. That old chestnut 'the more you tell, the more you sell' applies as much to a school fete as to double glazing.

So, be under no illusions – PR does not perform instant miracles. The Institute of Public Relations (IPR) has a very useful definition of PR: 'The *deliberate, planned and sustained* effort to establish and maintain mutual understanding between an organisation and its publics' (my italics).

Will your product stand the publicity?

Given that the publicity idea is worth the effort, you should next turn your mind to your 'product' (or whatever it is you are trying to promote).

Good PR could create enough interest to make somebody 'buy'

(or use, or subscribe to your organisation) *once*. But if your product, whatever it may be, is wrong, too bad. You can forget selling it to that person again.

Remember the Ford Edsel, the car that was launched on the US market with the best PR and advertising that money can buy? You don't? Well, join the club. Because the Edsel was a turkey, a failure of spectacular proportions. The car lives on today mainly as a case study to prove our point: the best PR in the world won't sell your product if that product is flawed. Not only that, but your attempts at PR, when the goods or services in question are not up to scratch, run the risk of failure – and on a spectacular scale.

It's worth pointing out that with a PR exercise, you are automatically handing over control of what actually appears in print to somebody else (ie, the media organisation concerned). That same media outlet you are trying to court always has the last say; it could easily turn the tables on you and reveal your attempts at 'image manufacturing' for what they are – effectively damning your product in the process.

A recent example is the way in which the *Sunday Times*, in a suitably 'campaigning' mood, took Westminster City Council to task for an alleged lack of litter removal facilities in the borough. 'Porter's dirty tactics' was the headline of a Comment piece, which was followed by an attack on the street-cleaning record of Westminster's Chairman, Lady Porter.

The tone of the piece went well beyond the fact that the *Sunday Times* thinks Westminster could be keeping the streets cleaner around London's showcase tourist spots, which is fair comment. Instead, it took this line:

> *The lady of this mucky manor [ie, Lady Porter] has come up with a 'clean' way of dealing with this unfortunate mess: public relations.*

> *Lady Porter's first response to the dirt was to hire Lowe Bell, the PR firm, to explain away the two-day-old discarded burger boxes and paper cups.*

This is the down-side of PR activity. The piece would have been less cutting if the PR agency had never been appointed in the first place.

But one swallow doesn't make a summer; PR is thankfully

about more ups than downs. And Westminster's PR agency would probably have been pleased to see an article which I spotted the very same week. This piece was in the *Westminster Post*, the local newspaper, circulating in the borough itself. Compare and contrast the *Sunday Times* piece with this:

> *Westminster is to splash out £500,000 on continental-style street washers and pavement sweepers.*
>
> *The machines can clean under cars, hose off graffiti and vacuum up dog mess and leaves. City Hall has also approved extra evening and weekend rubbish collections, more street washing, extending the Eurobin project and commissioning a design for special bins for street sweepers.*

The rest of the cutting was a lengthy quote concluding that: 'Westminster's streets will soon reflect the benefits of these improvements.' I strongly suspect that this piece was another of Lowe Bell's more successful PR efforts, and a worthy one at that (not least because of the targeting, of which more will be said in Chapter 2).

This example raises an interesting point; if the recognised PR professionals can come unstuck, what chance do you, the amateur, stand? And surely you need to be trained and have loads of contacts to work successfully on a PR campaign, or run the risk of the sort of pitfalls we have just illustrated?

How to make your PR campaign successful

Let's strip away a little of the mystique surrounding the world of PR. You don't need loads of contacts in the media world to generate media coverage. That said, they don't do any harm. But you will find that you quickly make your own working contacts the more you communicate with the journalists you deal with. However, you won't win a free plug on the air just because you recently sold, say, a lawn-mower to the presenter at your local TV station.

Every day, successful PR exercises are carried out in-house by small and medium-sized organisations, and there are column inches of print to prove the point. *Decent Exposure* will show you how they do it; the only things you need are the tips in this book and a bit of advanced planning.

Earlier, we looked at the IPR definition of PR, which explains the need for organisations to 'speak' to their publics. It's generally acknowledged that the most effective method of achieving this is through the mass media, which is why the term 'public relations' is often confused with a slightly different one, press relations.

In fact, the two are not synonymous; an effective PR campaign will have some elements that are beyond the reach of media exposure, which is, perforce, a broad brush. Likewise, a press relations exercise may not result in complete coverage, especially in the short term.

However, it is these two disciplines that dominate *Decent Exposure*; when your PR is right, you will automatically enjoy many side benefits in terms of customer relations and staff relations.

There is a school of thought that says PR is also useful in terms of parliamentary relations. Every MP I have ever known contributes to his or her local paper in some way, and there's a fair chance that they read them as well! So, although it may be the local media you wish to court, rather than the local party hierarchy, your PR successes could be noticed in the Commons.

By learning how journalists work, and understanding the various pressures they are continually under, you will avoid some of the most common problems facing the novice publicist.

Bear in mind that we are dealing with a less than scientific art, and one that relies heavily on other factors (including unexpected news events beyond anybody's control).

And here is our central premise: you have no automatic God-given right to free editorial exposure. Like most things worth having, you will need to put in a bit of effort, and 'goodwill' is a term which will be cropping up more than once. *Decent Exposure* will help you to increase your chances of success. Timing and treatment are both crucial factors; among other things, we will see how you can use other people's deadlines to your advantage.

One quick clarification before we continue: your PR exercises are not paid-for advertisements. If your message is unattractive to journalists as a news story or perhaps a softer 'feature' (using their criteria, not yours), then you are wasting everybody's time. It may well be that, if your message is boring but important enough, an ad will be the only solution. And you will need to budget accordingly for both time and cash.

For example, imagine you are an employer seeking a new member of staff. In itself, this is an unremarkable event, and any attempts to create free media coverage on the basis of this alone will almost certainly fail. Notice I avoid ruling it out altogether; if you run a circus and are seeking a new lion-tamer because your last one has just been eaten, you will probably succeed with little effort. However, for the rest of us, it will take a disproportionate amount of time and effort. It would be far easier all round simply to place an ad in the 'Situations Vacant' section of your local paper.

But supposing you run the ad for a month and you don't get a single response. *Now* you've got a possible news story on your hands, if you deal with it properly. You've probably seen similar stories yourself, normally along the lines of:

A Smallville boss has failed to attract a single worker from the town's estimated 2000 jobless.

Now Fred Skinflint of the High Street-based Ready Teddy toy company says he will be forced to go further afield to fill the vacancy. 'I need a production worker, or perhaps two, for our new Panda project. We need time to build up stock for the Christmas market', said 38-year-old Mr Skinflint.

Mr Skinflint will probably go on to comment on how surprised he is that he can't attract extra staff to his highly successful toy empire. No doubt he will point out that he is not seeking highly qualified staff, that flexitime is on offer, together with a bonus scheme etc; in other words, many of the elements of the original job ad.

The resultant piece will do well in terms of space in the local paper, especially if Mr Skinflint is prepared to pose for a picture with his bears at the factory.

However, there could be other factors involved; if he's only offering £50 for a 40-hour week, for example, it will be fairly obvious to the journalist covering the story why he's failed to attract applicants. The question 'How much are you paying?' is a legitimate one.

Assuming that the money offered is reasonable for the type of work in question, then this story will work. News hungry local reporters will give the subject far more prominence than the classified ad which Mr Skinflint had been paying for. Furthermore, if, by any chance, as a result of the story, the vacancy is filled, then the journalist can have a second bite at the cherry with this follow-up piece: 'Following a story in last week's *Echo*, a new worker has come forward . . .' etc.

This story is strong enough to transcend local newspaper boundaries (which you will quickly learn are crucial when you are placing stories). I once saw a cutting from a newspaper serving a town in the South East of England which was put there by a franchisor based in the Midlands, who was apparently having trouble attracting agents. The cutting even carried a phone number. What more could a frustrated entrepreneur ask?

Local newspapers are, by definition, parochial to the point of paranoia. If your proposed story hasn't got sufficient 'local' credibility, you will reduce its chances of being used. I have known reporters turn their nose up at a story from the adjacent village, saying its 'outside our area'. So, for our PR-conscious Brummie to score a hit in the South East is no mean achievement!

But PR is much more than a mere tool of marketing, or a sort of 'bolt-on goody' to add to your advertising as an afterthought. A recent poll carried out by MORI among senior industrialists proved this; apparently, around two-thirds (67 per cent) of the nation's captains of industry see PR more as a general management function than a specific marketing function.

That's an interesting insight, whether or not you are involved in the commercial world. And I have seen successful PR exercises carried out in the public sector, the voluntary sector and in politics, for example, using the same techniques every time. In short, PR is what you need it to be. And no matter what you are trying to promote – from accountancy to zoology – there is somebody, somewhere, who wants to hear about it. You just have to decide who they are and how best to reach them.

CHAPTER 2
The Power of Targeting

There is a very sensible rule of thumb that says before you can succeed at anything, you must establish what it is you are setting out to achieve. That's why the question 'What do you want to say?' is so important in creating free publicity opportunities, and forms the theme of this chapter. If you don't know, well, quite ·frankly, no one can tell you.

So, before we go into the nuts and bolts of self-promotion and free publicity, let's draw up our priorities by answering these three basic questions:

1. What do you want to say?
2. What do you hope to achieve by saying it?
3. Who do you want to say it to?

What do you want to say?

This first question, which we will call our *key message*, seems simple enough. But there's a catch. If asked, you could sit down and write a 5000-word treatise on the rationale of your organisation, and you'd probably do a cracking job. You would give a comprehensive and all-embracing answer, and produce the sort of paper that wins people a seat on the board. The problem is, you don't have the luxury of 5000 words. In fact, you only have about a dozen, so they had better be good!

It's not impossible, but it does require a sensitive and succinct approach; verbosity, minute detail and self-important hot air are *out*; a combination of concise expression and clarity of thought are *in*.

You're probably thinking to yourself, how can a mere dozen words possibly explain what a splendid company you are running and give enough detail of your impressive range of products? Well, have a go anyway. If you are going to make your organisation headline news, it will be an invaluable start if you can introduce yourself to the discipline of thinking in headlines (or something very close). Brevity at this stage will pay dividends, not only in your press releases but also in the radio and television interviews that follow.

So, if you can't fit your answer to this and the other two questions on the back of an envelope, then try again until you can. (A handy back-of-an-envelope substitute is provided here for ready reference so that you won't have to tear out your hair trying to find the original one when it has disappeared with all your carefully selected *bons mots* on the back.)

If you get stuck on your key message, try this experiment: imagine you have to send a telex to a potential customer telling him or her all they need to know in less than a dozen words. Not only that, but the fewer words you take to do the job, the greater your chances of winning the business. If you aim for something approaching 'Beans Meanz Heinz' you won't go far wrong!

If you are considering hiring a PR agency to work with you, it will prepare answers to these basic questions as part of its brief. If the agency's interpretation of what you are after fails to include answers to these three basic questions somewhere, then you should be talking to another PR agency. Given that you are working without a third party, however, you will need to have these answers to hand throughout the execution of your PR programme.

Obviously, the 'envelope answers' will vary enormously depending on the requirements of your own organisation. No matter who you are or what you do, you really need some sort of strategy; these answers provide as good a basis as any for an individual communication programme.

1. What do you want to say? (Key message)

....

....

2. What do you hope to achieve by saying it?

....

....

3. Who do you want to say it to? (Target markets)

....

....

What do you hope to achieve by saying it?

Now you have your concise key message, let's take a look at this second question. The first part of the answer is self-explanatory; you want a journalist to 'do a piece' on it, or at least to be sufficiently interested to find out more about your organisation. Then come the important strategic elements. Are you looking to introduce a new product to a crowded market, perhaps? Or are you hoping to launch a new service and attract new customers? Perhaps you have a special event coming up and you want to attract an audience. In each case, you are hoping that publicity will help you to achieve new business for your organisation. Alternatively, your goal could be more basic – simply to get your organisation's name noticed by the people you are currently dealing with (or, perhaps, hope to deal with at some future point). This alone is no mean achievement. Mae West, the sultry screen goddess once said: 'I don't care what they say about me as long as they spell my name right.'

Who do you want to say it to?

PR is often a broad brush. If media relations are to carry your message home successfully, not only do you need a concise key message with a specific purpose behind it, you also need to know precisely who you want to read/hear it. It stands to reason, therefore, that you should take some time to find out who reads what. That's where our third question comes in.

Suppose you are setting up a youth club in your town for the first time. You have identified a target 'market' – 11–16 year olds – and you have decided that it is these young people you want to reach. Now, how do you get to them?

There would be no point in attempting to get a mention for the club in the *Financial Times*. You would fail anyway, because the FT journalists know their readership, which does not include many 11–16 year olds, let alone 11–16 year olds in the town where your youth club is planned.

But supposing you forget the national press and concentrate on your local media. Using your carefully targeted press release (of which more will be said in Chapter 3) you could interest the local newspaper in running a feature about you and your ideas for the club.

This is a much better approach, because you have targeted a local media outlet which covers the area you are looking to establish. Many mums and dads buy the weekly paper or at least flick through the freesheet that arrives through their door. In some areas, of course, the weekly freesheet may be the only newspaper with local news – such titles are no longer the 'poor relation' of their paid-for opposition titles that they were when they first appeared. The point is, some local readers are parents who may have a vested interest in persuading junior to join your club, if only so they know where he or she is some of the time!

Let's take the idea a stage further. Suppose you want to reach the target market itself rather than the target market's parents. Such an approach is more difficult still, as the average 11–16 year old does not tend to read the local press as closely as parents do (although he or she may be responsible for delivering it). This is where some lateral thinking could provide the answer. The average 11–16 year old may not read a lot of local material but he or she does tend to listen to the local commercial radio station. Independent local radio (ILR) stations tend to have a young and highly regionalised audience.

The Radio Marketing Bureau (RMB) has produced a useful booklet, *Radio: the Facts*, in which it is claimed that independent local radio will typically reach 60 per cent of 15–19 year olds. This little booklet will save you a lot of legwork. It gives total UK radio coverage, station by station, area by area, and includes addresses and telephone numbers. You can find out what your local station is (as opposed to the one you happen to pick up when the wind is blowing in the right direction), the number of listeners it has and the listeners as a percentage of the total population. At times, the advertising and marketing orientation of the booklet can be off-putting, but it is well worth getting hold of a copy nevertheless. In all fairness, the RMB is a specialist organisation which aims to persuade those in the advertising industry of the power of independent radio.

In fact, the advertising industry puts much emphasis on your third answer, the one about targeting; continual market research goes into checking that the 'right people' are getting the right message. Within our limited resources, we too must try to adopt a targeted approach for our drive.

But please be realistic. I have heard the targeting argument taken too far. I once worked with an account executive at an advertising agency who argued that my attempts to reach the readership of a particular national newspaper were pointless. If you are trying to promote something which is strictly local (and a niche within the local 'universe' at that), he argued, what is the point of creating favourable coverage in a national title? What he had overlooked was the fact that some of the local target market will also read that national newspaper. And national exposure could lead to fresh enquiries from other niches which could only be of interest to our client. Plus, and this really closed the argument for me, the fact that local journalists often follow up stories that have been in the nationals, trying to find new 'angles' to make their story even more interesting. (In Chapter 9, we will see that this is a two-way street, as local journalists also provide the stories that the national press use first.)

If your story is strong enough, it will work for you in both the local and the national press. This joint objective should be our PR goal. One will effectively reinforce the other. The same applies to the trade press, and these three different media sectors (local, national and trade) should be in the back of your mind whenever you are considering PR possibilities.

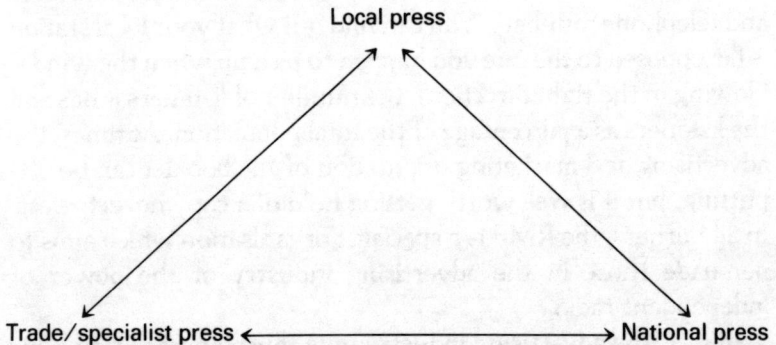

Local press

Trade/specialist press ← → National press

There is 'traffic' between the three written-press sectors; a story in one could be picked up and developed/reworked in another.

In all fairness, my colleague from the advertising agency was used to spending his client's hard-earned cash on each insert, and so he was as choosy and objective as possible. You will not be in such a position. Your coverage will be free, so you will want as much of it as you can get, wherever you can get it. This is one of the fundamental differences between advertising and PR: a good story about your organisation is never wasted on any audience.

I once worked for a company producing tyres and rubber goods. Two of the workers coming up to retirement had been with the company for 50 years, which in itself was no mean achievement. But there was an extra 'human interest' story. The two workers were twin brothers, and they were more than happy to co-operate with the local photographers as they finished their last shift together. The company press release, and the subsequent coverage that resulted from it, probably didn't help to sell a single tyre. But readers of the local press (and, later, those tuned to their local radio and TV stations) saw that the company was a 'human' one to work for, and the sort of firm that could keep employees for half a century at a stretch. In Chapter 3, we will go into 'human interest' in more detail; at this point, it is enough to say that the story about the retiring twins could help to make subsequent recruitment in that area just that little bit easier.

Without labouring the point, the 'target' behind the press release was not, therefore, the people who would buy the tyres that the twins had made, but rather the people in the community who could be (or are already) employees. So, the concept of targeting is a useful one *in moderation*. It certainly pays to ask: Who do you want to reach and will this PR exercise help to reach them?

For those in the business of marketing fast-moving consumer goods (or FMCG as it is constantly referred to), a 'science' has been developed as the media outlets themselves have grown and fragmented. Specific requirements of advertisers are now mirrored effectively by the commercial media seeking the revenue (via the third party, the advertising agency). We have already seen how commercial radio stations go about wooing potential clients, and national magazines also offer quite detailed profiles of their readership for the same reason.

In the past, people were happy to talk in the broadest of terms, using expressions like 'women's press', but this doesn't work today. Now a more hard-nosed, fragmented marketing edge has crept in.

OK, the 'women's press' may all have 'women' as their primary target readers, but such a profile is not good enough. What sort of women? How old are they? And (predictably) what do they buy? Also bear in mind that such magazines have a very long lead time, so your proposed news item must not have a limited 'shelf-life'.

Here are some extracts from a digest of IPC magazines to illustrate the point about the range within the readership:

Young profile, with a bias towards 18–34, which accounts for 40 per cent of the readership. Interests: fashion, special offers. Higher disposable income with a group reading a number of magazines interested in life-style improvements.

Woman's Own

Slightly older profile, with a bias towards 20–40, accounting for 43 per cent of the readership. Interests: fashion, parent care, middle to up-market leisure goods and services.

Woman

Older profile, with a bias towards the 40–65 age group. Interests include cookery, home improvement, hobbies and crafts.

Woman's Realm (ABC Jan–Jun 1985: 636,984)

High bias towards 40–65+, amounting to 47 per cent of the readership. Profile is of women who enjoy cookery and hobbies.

Woman's Weekly (ABC Jan–Jun 1987: 1.3 million)

A very high bias towards 55+ female age range, with a B/C1/C2 socio-economic grade. People who very much enjoy a range of hobbies, particularly cooking.

Woman and Home

High bias towards A/B/C1/C2, with an average age range of 15–34. Interests include cooking, knitting, sewing, handicrafts, gardening, decorating or home improvement.

Essentials

As you can see from the list, age is a factor, as are interests. Also, the circulation details of the magazines could be useful background for you, as determined by the Audit Bureau of Circulations (the ABC), an independent body that keeps accurate records of the numbers of issues sold by certain titles.

The breakdown goes further still. Socio-economic groupings are cited specifically in the entries for *Woman and Home* and *Essentials*. There are six basic categories (A, B, C1, C2, D and E) into which all consumers fit (and, at the risk of confusing things further, these categories have nothing whatsoever to do with the ABC of the Audit Bureau of Circulations mentioned earlier).

Much loved by both the sociologist and those involved with a commercial variant called 'demographics', the socio-economic theory can be summarised thus: those at the upper end of the social scale (and, therefore, those who apparently have the most disposable income) are A/B/C1s, while those further down the scale (C2/D/Es) have less spare cash for consumer spending.

But leaving the socio-economic grouping to one side, there is plenty of food for thought in the IPC magazine list. For example, it stands to reason that if you are marketing garden rakes (with women purchasers in mind), the advice would be to try and get a mention in *Essentials*, as that would seem to have more potential (women) garden rake buyers than the other magazines in the women's weekly stable at IPC. In terms of your press release list (see Chapter 3), however, such information is only of limited use.

Knowledge of your 'target media' becomes even more important when you are in a position to offer 'exclusives' and to do deals with certain journalists.

The easiest way to check the 'readership profile' of a publication is to find the title in *Willings Press Guide*. *Willings*, which at the time of writing has published more than 115 annual updates, has a 'subject interest grouping', which effectively helps you by putting together a list of all your 'target titles'. Then, in individual listings, it provides the name of the editor, the addresses you need and circulation details. *Willings* is nothing if not comprehensive; the 1989 edition boasted over 11,000 UK newspapers, periodicals and annuals, everything from *AA* (a monthly magazine which deals with business and financial management, aimed at accountants) to *Zzap 64* (another monthly aimed at owners of Commodore 64s interested in computer games). *Willings* is a useful reference book, but perhaps not one you need by you constantly; most libraries stock the current copy in the 'Reference' section.

However, I do recommend that you actually invest in another specialist title, *The Writers' and Artists' Yearbook*, which describes itself as the 'indispensable handbook for writers, artists, etc'. Although the *Yearbook* does not go into circulation details in the same way as *Willings*, it does provide a short listing for every title included. These few words can be invaluable; they will tell you, at a glance, what the editorial team is looking for.

As you may have guessed, the *Yearbook* exists to help writers to sell their work to editors. So you can see what the publications not only seek, but are prepared to pay for!

The question of payment is academic in your case. The convention is that freelance journalists are rightly reimbursed for their professionally produced editorial material. Your material, however, is provided to the publication free of charge; your only reward will be seeing your story in print.

Until recently, the same applied to radio and television, but these days the demarcation is not nearly so clear. If you appear and perform (for performing is what it is) on your local TV evening news, you probably won't be offered an appearance fee. Authors of books are also expected to appear on a show for free, the tacit agreement being that they will have ample opportunity to 'plug the book'. But this promotional game is an increasingly subtle one, as illustrated by the following example.

Certain video production companies recently considered charging the BBC for using their material on shows such as *Top of the Pops*. The BBC responded, with all its corporate pomp, by pointing out that these pop videos were essentially 'promos', designed to sell records for their artists, and that the companies should be grateful that the BBC was showing them at all. The production companies struck to their guns and argued that, were it not for the broadcast quality videos they were providing, the BBC would have to pay the same artistes for appearing live on the programme and so incur production costs to fill the same airwaves.

This incident illustrates the way in which the media and the publicist have a curious mutual dependency. Back in the print world, this can be expressed in crude business terms. The editor of your specialist trade magazine probably needs you (and your editorial material, if it's suitable) as much as you need him or her. What makes your editorial suitable is its relevance to the readership (targeting), its timing (targeting again), and its news value. These three elements are crucial, but so too is the format you use to present them, which is where the press release comes in.

CHAPTER 3
Tackling the First Press Release

What you don't see

The key to successful press relations, the press release, is a device much maligned by journalists who have to deal with too many bad examples of the genre. Also referred to as a 'hand-out' or a 'news release', most end up in the bin or, worse still, the subject of cruel jibes from impatient editors. One business magazine I used to see from time to time actually ran a regular feature called 'Worst press release of the week'. But, fortunately, such antics are exceptional.

What you don't see is far more typical: how most journalists will shamelessly use good, informative press releases verbatim. And, sometimes, press releases are actually presented to unknowing readers as the journalist's own work, complete with the 'writer's' name or byline at the top. If this should ever happen to one of your press releases, then you know you have arrived. Anonymous you may be, but you will have the satisfaction of knowing that your material has emerged victorious from the hundreds of badly written attempts that arrive at media offices daily.

National newspapers, the trade press, radio stations and television news rooms are literally bombarded with these things. And, without exaggeration, over 90 per cent of them never see the light of day. A waste of time, and, of course, paper.

As both a reporter 'consuming' them, and later as an originator putting them together from scratch, I am convinced that there are three main factors which will determine whether or not your press release will end up as headlines, or destined for the shredder:

1. Targeting
2. Timing
3. Quality of writing.

As we have already looked closely at the power of targeting in Chapter 2, this chapter is primarily intended to help you to focus on timing and quality of writing.

It's worth reiterating one point at this stage: you should always choose your media outlets with care. Before you send out any press release, you need to consider two things:

1. Will the outlet want to use the story?
2. Will the story do you some good in this particular medium?

If your answer to both these questions is yes, then the chances are that your press release will be very welcome. Not only will the piece stand a good chance of interesting the reader/listener/viewer, but it will also help the editor/reporter to fill his or her column inches (or airwaves, of course) without too much hard work.

Timing your press release

The precise timing of the arrival of your press release can be crucial. So, remember to use the directories to establish when a publication is due to appear, and make sure you build in a suitable lead time.

Most local weekly papers are understandably reluctant to include material which is effectively ten days old. So, if your story/press release doesn't reach the news room until, say, Wednesday afternoon, you may have missed the deadline for that week, albeit by only a couple of hours. But a miss is a miss, and that week's paper (which will appear typically on the Friday) cannot carry your press release. In newspaper jargon, the paper has already 'gone to bed'.

In such cases, the best you can hope for is that your story is strong enough to last from that Wednesday afternoon until

Friday week, but it loses a lot of its 'news appeal' in the meantime. Editors want their papers to carry 'news', not 'has-beens'. Your story is competing for a coveted space against news stories and features which editors must carry (because they have a short shelf-life, or for legal reasons in the case of court reports). A weak or 'iffy' story will get a better treatment if it is 'on-hand' for inclusion on what is known as an 'early' page (ie, one which is put together well before the newspaper deadline pressure starts to mount).

Some media outlets may decide to 'dig a bit' around a press release to see if they can make it more interesting. But this takes time, and time is precious when you have a deadline to meet. More often than not, the newspaper reporters or sub-editors dealing with your press release will slightly rework the text, adding their own inimitable style in order to conform with house rules. Quite often, they will cut it right down to the first paragraph, which they can then fit nearly into a 'News In Brief' (NIB) column; hence the need to keep the intro concise and self-contained.

Minor stylistic modifications aside, you can now see why it's far better for all concerned if your press release can stand alone. If the story you are offering is strong, relevant to the audience and well timed, there is every possibility that it will be used, probably word for word. And you will have achieved your objective: generating free editorial coverage for your key message.

There are other methods of generating interest from a journalist: personal contact is, of course, also good. But remember, you are working against the news room clock. Your idea in a vague, conversational form over the phone will require some concentration from a journalist, who may resist making a commitment for fear that there isn't much of a story at the end of it. And if you sound anything at all like a waffle merchant, the reporter or editor you have managed to reach will ask, in the nicest possible way, where's the beef? If you do not have a good story to tell, and quickly, you may as well save your breath and your phone bill.

Thus, the beauty of the press release: they read it first, then they ring you if they're interested. Before they even lift up the phone, they already have a fair idea what they are talking about . . . thanks to your carefully prepared hard work.

The timing principle applies to evening/daily newspapers as well as weeklies. Early editions of the evening papers are often on the street at lunch-time, so when you think about it, the first editorial deadline will be fairly early in the morning (bearing in mind margins for printing, delivery etc). I know of at least one columnist on a provincial evening paper who refuses to talk to you before 10.30 am, no matter what story you are touting. It's not because he's rude – he has a good reason, in fact. Not only does he write his column, he also doubles up as a sub-editor, struggling to get the first edition out. After 10.30 am, when the first deadline of the day has been effectively dealt with, he is happy to work on your story with you.

So, you have to get up fairly early in the morning to get a story into the first edition of an evening paper. And it may sound unlikely, but certain major evening papers actually welcome picture calls at around 8 am. This is not because their photographers are insomniacs, but because they can use the resulting picture in their first edition, so effectively 'beating' the national dailies (which, of course, won't appear until the next morning).

Daily papers, on the other hand, are produced at night. Their journalists have all day to get their act together, as their final deadline for pictures and copy may not be until nearly 11 pm. But even among the national titles, deadlines vary considerably; factors such as the production methods, location of the print-works and train times to various parts of the country are all relevant. This is why some of the nationals will be able to accommodate a story which 'breaks' late at night and still get it on to the breakfast tables across the country. On the other hand, those with a slightly earlier deadline will miss it and have to be content to carry it the following morning – again, only if it's strong enough. Pride normally dictates whether some extra editorial labour is put into finding a new 'angle' on a story that the other papers managed to squeeze in the day before.

The equation becomes even more complicated when the nationals produce 'regionalised' versions of their paper. Typically, these will be very similar to those across the country, with the exception of local TV listings, choice of regional sports reports and some local news or pictures.

These finer points of timing, as they apply to train times and print schedules, are not really your worry. Suffice it to say, don't try to get your story to the news rooms of the nationals at midnight; unless you have something quite amazing to offer, you are not helping yourself or anybody else. If you are a lover of that hoary newspaper cliché 'Hold the front page', then I had better disabuse you immediately. The expression, although not unheard of, almost certainly does not apply to your PR stories; your job is to find out the deadlines and work well within them, so increasing your chances of success with your press release.

Writing your press release

So, what exactly *is* a press release? How should you write one? Where should it go? How can you avoid yours joining the vast majority of rejects?

Quite simply, a press release is a document written in such a way as to provide the media 'customer' with enough information to write a piece for a newspaper (or provide the basis of a script or 'treatment' for radio or TV).

It can be as short as just two or three carefully worded paragraphs, or it can be as long as perhaps three pages of A4. But these tend to be the exceptions at either end of the spectrum. Most news room journalists, who are normally on the receiving end of press releases, pride themselves on concise expression. It's almost an obsession with the tabloid boys, who hate wasted words at the best of times. And, although it is unlikely that you will ever see it written down, most journalists slaving over a hot VDU tend to follow a blunt philosophy: the news story has not happened that could not be told in ten paragraphs.

Some sub-editors argue that even the Bible could be reworked, to a dozen or so tightly constructed paragraphs. That's taking things a bit far, but in terms of day-to-day news, they probably have a point. If your first press release adopts this structure, or something approaching it, you are greatly improving its chance of success.

A typical press release will be no longer than two pages of A4. If you haven't told your story by the end of the second page, it is unlikely that you ever will. Most press releases follow these conventions:

Format

They are *always* typed, on one side of the paper only, with 1½ or double spacing. There is normally a generous margin (2" or so) on one or both sides. This isn't a waste of paper; it's there for a purpose – or, at least, it was.

Until recent years, a sub-editor on a newspaper or magazine used these margins and the space in between lines to mark up your press release as 'copy'; in other words, to annotate it for the printers to work with, complete with notes stating typeface and column widths etc. Speed was the reason why only one side of the paper was used; the theory was that copy could be cut and pasted so that individual compositors (or 'comps') could work on various parts of the story simultaneously, saving valuable minutes before the presses started rolling. But with the dawn of information technology in most news rooms, this part of the process is redundant. 'Subbing' tends to happen on screen as part of the direct input (DI) process. The conventions live on, however, partly because that's what conventions tend to do, and partly because radio and TV journalists can use the space on press releases for cue notes and so on.

Intro

The intro (first paragraph) is the heart of the press release. Within the first paragraph, you must set out your stall: you should include the news story, part of your key message (as outlined in Chapter 2) and enough spark or interest to make journalists (and their readers) want to read on. If you think that's a tall order, that's just the half of it. The whole thing should be no more than 30 words, and ideally a single sentence. Remember, *every* word must count.

Two further points about the intro. First, because of the sheer bulk of rubbish pushed across the news desk, the intro is about all that gets read most of the time. Those first 30 words will, therefore, determine whether your work will sink or swim.

Second, the intro should be, as near as possible, self-contained. If all the elements just mentioned are included, then an editor can effectively cut out the rest of the press release altogether. Yes, I know, your other carefully crafted nine paragraphs may be wasted. But if the most important one gets into print, more or less as you wrote it, then the others have not given their lives in vain, and you have no cause for complaint, either.

Remember, your press release is effectively saving a journalist the job of researching, interviewing somebody and writing. So, your intro should try to answer the 'big six' questions that journalists always want to cover. Kipling summed these up neatly enough:

> I keep six honest serving-men
> (They taught me all I knew)
> Their names are What and Why and When
> And How and Where and Who.

Points of style

Paper
You may be tempted to use your normal letter-head as press release paper. You do, however, create a better impression by having a special version printed exclusively for the purpose. Either way, the words 'press release' or 'press information' plus your logo or name must be on the front sheet, at the top, written fairly large. Also, typed nearby, should be the date and some sort of headline.

The question of the role of the headline is rather controversial. It's an important label for your story, but some argue that it is a waste of time because, more often than not, your chosen headline will not be used, even if the story itself wins a space. Fair comment; sub-editors have enough constraints on their layout without your attempts at headlines to add to them.

However, it is still a good discipline; you never know, it may just 'fit' the space left for a heading at the top of the printed article. And once you have decided on a headline, the rest of the press release will flow more easily than if you start from scratch with a blank sheet of paper.

Layout

Paragraphs should not be 'broken' from one sheet to the next; end each paragraph neatly on the same page you started it, and at the bottom of the page state either 'continued' or 'more follows' (sometimes abbreviated to MF). When using MF, the end of the press release should state (logically enough) 'ends'. In the text itself, spell out numbers from one to nine but use figures for 10 and above.

Contact

Give a contact for further information, with name and telephone number, at the very end of the press release, and divorce these details from the main text. This information is meant primarily for the recipient (ie, not designed for publication), although some smaller trade association-type newsletters have been known to print these details as well.

Use of language

As a rule of thumb, you should write your press release in the style of a 'mid-brow' title (à la *Today*, *Daily Express* and *Daily Mail*). In other words, a common-sense approach to your choice of language; not too up-market or punctuated with technical allusions (like, say, the *Financial Times*) but also avoiding the other extreme – tabloid-style slang and puns.

Press release checklist

Here is a checklist – 'the seven Ps' – for drafting your first press release. Read through the checklist and then have a go. If your mind is a total blank, read on; two ideas are provided for you to choose from to get you started.

Does your press release:

1. *Provoke* because it's interesting? It may be an announcement, a launch, a revelation, a development or a surprise, but it *must* be novel, or newsworthy. And not just to those in your organisation, but to the public at large. If not, don't bother sending it out, because it won't be used.
2. Explore the possibility of a *picture* opportunity?
3. Allow access to a *personality* – someone who can be interviewed, or at least quoted in your press release?
4. *Phrase* your key message in an unambiguous way – realistic and non-sloganistic?
5. *Pitch* itself correctly at your target media/market? Remember, in an ideal world, each media outlet will have its own customised press release.
6. *Provide* answers to the six basic questions – *who, what, why, where, when* and *how*? If not in your first paragraph, then as soon as possible.
7. Have a *phone* number for further information and follow-up?

Two golden oldies to think about

Chapter 7 outlines some 'tried and tested' stories which almost every organisation can use to its advantage if it is seeking a steady supply of 'decent exposure'. Two such 'stock' stories, for want of a better expression, are here so that you can use them in conjunction with the press release checklist to produce a first written draft.

Whether you plan to draft something yourself from scratch, or draw on one of these two golden oldies, remember to follow these basic rules:

- Ten paragraphs, maximum.
- One thought per sentence.
- No more than 30 words in your intro.
- Make every word work hard – aim for brevity/simplicity.

New faces
This is the classic human interest story. Mr X or Ms Y has been appointed to a new job within your organisation. He or she may

be a new recruit, someone promoted internally or simply someone changing roles. The story could win a space in everything from the *Farnham Herald* to the *Financial Times* (subject to your targeting).

In each case, your press release should include the full name and age of the appointee, brief details of the new job, the title the person will now take and, to round it off, some selected biographical material. Include previous jobs, unusual hobbies/interests, any special position in the community, if the person is married/single etc.

Within your press release, allow room for a reasonable quote (two good paragraphs or so) from the appointee. It is suggested that you draft the quote and then give it to the appointee for approval. By doing this, you can keep it reasonably tight and avoid any ego-merchants getting too carried away! You may also choose, of course, to take the opportunity to reinforce part of your key message in a human (as opposed to corporate) way.

Tip: It pays to target your local media with care if you decide to do a 'new faces' story, as you could get two bites of the cherry.

Remember, local papers are strictly local; if your appointee will be working in Northtown but actually lives in Southtown, then do two slightly different versions of the same press release, pushing the local angle in each case. So, 'Southtown woman has been appointed as . . .' will be the intro for the press release destined for the *Southtown Gazette*, while 'The Northtown-based grommet company has announced a new appointment . . .' will go down better with the *Northtown Chronicle*.

Your 'new faces' press release will stand a much better chance of being used if you actually send out a black-and-white picture with it (see Chapter 5).

If you haven't appointed anybody new, don't worry about it. You could still use this format if somebody who has been with you for a while takes on a new title. It could be that one of the sales managers in your organisation has been briefed specifically to explore the opportunities of the Single European Market in 1992, when 320 million consumers will be able to buy and sell from each other without trade restrictions. There is no reason why you can't put together a draft press release reflecting this important (and topical) move. Your intro could read something like this:

> *Tommy Bloggs has been appointed European Sales Manager at the Northtown Grommet Company with the brief to prepare for 1992.*
>
> *Bloggs, 45, will continue with his present overseas sales duties, supplying grommets to such distant countries as Australia and North America.*

Survey story

Used to great effect by retail outlets such as Tie Rack, the survey story is literally that – brief conclusions (as interesting/novel as you can make them) of a survey which your organisation has carried out. The Tie Rack survey, which secured column inches in several of the nationals, focused on the colours preferred according to 'type' of customer; red ties tended to be the choice of extroverts, blue ties by (small c) conservatives etc.

The scope of such stories is endless. Here are a couple of (fictitious) examples of survey story intros:

> More than *eight out of ten motorists in Northtown have now converted their vehicles to lead-free petrol, say High Street car dealers Honest Johns* . . .
>
> Less than *2 per cent of adult men now have their suits tailor made, a recent survey has revealed. Carried out on behalf of the Southtown-based menswear chain, Sharpsuits, the survey shows that expense is still a major drawback for the not-so-dedicated follower of fashion* . . .

Obviously, the cost of actually commissioning the survey is partially offset by the free PR that follows. Market research companies will quote you for a range of basic surveys/research; addresses for market research companies are listed in the *Yellow Pages*.

Without going too far into the methodology of market research, there are two techniques that are particularly relevant for your PR purposes:

1. *An omnibus.* This is a large survey, done regularly, which you can buy into. The questionnaire may consist of 50 questions, and there could be potentially 50 different organisations

'buying in'. So, the topics could be quite diverse. The ir.terviewees could be asked anything from 'What brand of fish fingers do you buy?' to 'Are you a member of a health club?'

With such surveys, you receive feedback *only* on your question(s). An omnibus survey is relatively cheap, and quick (typically a two-week turn-round, so your press release will be nothing if not topical). In addition, it can be quite specialised; for example, a sample of 1000 women, or 1000 boys under 16, or 1000 business executives.

2. *Syndicated research.* In this type of market research, you buy into a survey along with other people who are interested in the same things as you. The drawback is that the information you receive from the market research agency will be common knowledge to all these other people, some of whom could be your competitors, and consequently they will know a little more about what you are doing. On the other hand, you can pay to have your own 'private' questions added, which will provide data that only you will see.

Tip: Do you already have statistical evidence of your market share for a particular product/service? If so, you could do a survey story without commissioning market research. However, choose your material with care: you don't want to give out any 'market-sensitive' material for the sake of a few glowing lines and a name check!

CHAPTER 4
What They Need . . .
How You Provide It

Advertising revenue - the other side of the publicity coin

Journalists need good stories, but their publishers have slightly different priorities. Interesting editorial material is important, but so too are buoyant circulation figures and a healthy flow of advertising revenue to pay the bills.

So, from the boss's point of view, editorial material, especially the sort that sells extra copies, is useful, mainly as a means to a profitable end. Each title has to fight its corner in a competitive market, and every publisher (big or small) has to keep a close eye on the bottom line. This doesn't just apply to newspapers; the same goes for magazines and independent local radio stations. Leaving aside the BBC for a moment, let us turn our attention to the sensitive question of cash, or, to be more specific, advertising revenue, as it affects TV, radio, newspapers and magazines.

We've already seen how PR is concerned largely with finding ways to persuade people to write about your organisation or firm without any payment. But nobody has ever made their first million as a media baron by relying entirely on good stories from nice people like you, and printing them free of charge.

So, with our feet firmly on the ground, we have to overcome the conventional sensitivity about money and consider briefly the other, paid-for, side of the publicity coin.

At the risk of contradicting myself straight away, I have two quite different messages to give you here. The first, which we have already touched on, is the fact that most journalists pride themselves on their editorial independence and integrity. We have seen how attempts to persuade a reporter to write about you simply because you are advertising in his or her newspaper will almost certainly fail. Nine times out of ten, the reporter/news editor will decide whether or not your story is any good on the strength of the story alone, regardless of your advertising budget, or lack of it. To my mind, this is one of the beauties of PR: a little bit of creativity on your part will pay you dividends; no hefty advertising budget is needed. Incidentally, journalists on the better freesheets, which are circulated with no cover charge whatsoever, guard their editorial independence just as jealously as their colleagues on the paid-for rival publications.

My second point, almost by way of total contradiction, is that smaller magazines (especially those distributed free to a limited, controlled readership) depend entirely on advertising. So, it isn't surprising that the publisher-cum-editor of a little-known magazine (which might only employ an editor and an advertising salesperson) may well make promises about 'free' editorial space if you agree to buy advertising space in the next issue. Quite how this proposal is put to you will vary. You might, for example, have sent your press release to the news editor of a specific magazine which in turn leads to a phone call, not from the news room, but from the advertising department. The voice on the line will tell you in one breath that *Gumshield Monthly* is interested in running your story while asking you in the next breath if you would be interested in taking out an advert to go with it, at a suitably discounted rate, of course.

The decision is yours. However, you would be well advised to make it on advertising considerations alone. There is no reason why your press release, if it is carefully crafted and tailor made for the *Gumshield Monthly* readership, should fail to win an (editorial) space in its own right. So, with this in mind, your response to the advertising rep should be equally businesslike. Without committing yourself, ask to see the media pack for the magazine, complete with the 'rate card' (cost of advertising space). In addition, as a direct approach has been made, rather than through an advertising agency, ask if you can have the agency discount (which is normally about 10 per cent of the rate card) price. *Resist* pressure sales talk, trying to wring an immediate decision from you there and then, in order to meet a 'deadline'. If the magazine is good, there will be another issue next month, won't there?

If, after careful consideration, you feel that the magazine is worth an ad, then by all means go ahead. But don't agree to take out an ad solely on the 'nod and a wink' of a commission-hungry sales rep. The editorial decision about your press release may not be his or hers to make at the end of the day and you may be disappointed.

Advertorials

Sometimes the dividing line between 'editorial' and 'advertising' becomes more blurred. For example, a local newspaper may contact you to find out if you would be interested in taking part in an advertising feature. Such features are known in the agency world as 'advertorials'. They consist of an agreed editorial space surrounded by advertising, some of which is from your organisation, some from your suppliers etc.

The standard of advertorials can vary enormously. The contact is likely to be from the advertising department, not the editorial section/news room. The sales rep might persuade you to send in an extra copy of your latest press release, which can then easily form the basis of the advertisement feature. It should state somewhere (normally on the top of the page) that it is an 'advertising feature', so it can be distinguished from a straightforward editorial.

The strength of the advertorial is that you can insist that your material goes in verbatim (as the editorial space is actually part of the deal). Editorially, of course, this means far more control than usual; your press release therefore escapes running the usual gauntlet of reporter/news editor/sub-editor, and you can demand that your material goes in precisely as it left you. The same goes for pictures: their selection and treatment within the advertorial will be left largely to you.

Sometimes the advertising department will offer to arrange for a journalist to work on the advertorial on your behalf. This can be useful, but if you have a healthy supply of editorial material (ie, stock press releases of your own) it may not be necessary. Also, the journalist will want to be paid extra for writing your copy. This cost may be hidden by the sales rep during the negotiations, but don't forget, at the end of the day, you will have to pay for the extra pair of hands, one way or another.

If you *do* decide to use a journalist to act as your advertorial writer, then *insist* on seeing what he or she proposes putting together on your behalf. Remember, he who pays the piper etc. It's as well to clarify this from the outset.

I once took on an advertorial for a client and asked a staff journalist to work with us on the project. Although he was effectively doing advertorials 'on the side', he refused point blank to show me what he intended writing about my client. Now, of course, that's fine when he is working for his news editor, and you will have to respect that. But when he's taking cash from a client to write a supplement to some advertising, then different rules apply.

I raised the matter with the advertising manager and told him quite simply that I would advise my client to pull out of the whole exercise unless we had advance sight of what the writer was planning on putting in. He had a word with the reluctant wordsmith, with the result that all was sweetness and light once more. I suspect that the reason I got such immediate co-operation was largely due to the fact that the advertising manager knew that his team had been successfully selling 'supporting' advertising – and, without us, there was no feature to support!

One last thought about advertorials. There is always a nagging doubt that you might be effectively paying through the nose for a space which you may have secured free of charge elsewhere in the same newspaper, using your editorial skills. This is made all the more acute by the way the sales rep will try to winkle out of you all the names you can provide, and then approach them to sell extra space around the feature.

It is highly unlikely that these punters will get any 'editorial' space; they will have to settle for an ad somewhere in the feature, bathing in your reflected glory. Nevertheless, you may find it galling having to do some of the work for the sales rep. What's in it for you if he or she happens to sell a space to your suppliers?

The other drawback is the fact that your material is surrounded by ads which, frankly, are produced on a budget. Design (ie, the page layout) will always come a poor second when there is extra advertising revenue to be squeezed out of an advertorial.

Layout
Here are a few tips regarding layout of your advertorial. First, if you are going for a two-page spread, ask to have your own ad (not the editorial-style material but the advert itself) in the bottom right-hand corner. This is the prime spot; newspaper folk generally accept that the eye tends to fall on the right-hand page when a newspaper is opened. And as it's your advertising feature, you should have first choice of ad position.

Second, do a little 'guide' for the people putting the feature together. You don't need anything elaborate: state (roughly) where you want which bits of the editorial and/or pictures to go and thus save disappointment when the work has already been done. Mark your copy 'page lead' or 'mid-page', for example, and sketch out very roughly what you see going where. Your precise requirements will hopefully end up in the hands of the person handling the page layout, which will help him or her and you. Lastly, insist on seeing a 'proof' (ie, the finished layout before it is printed in the paper).

Large-scale alterations should not be embarked on at proof stage, but you are entitled to check for literals (typography errors) which should be corrected – at the newspaper's expense, not yours. At the end of the day, it's your organisation's public image at stake, so you want to be sure you are happy with what gets printed.

Drawbacks
Although advertorials have their place, they are to be tolerated rather than encouraged. By going down the advertorial road you are losing out on one of the primary advantages of PR. Be honest now, which do you find the more credible in a printed publication: the adverts, with all their glossy hype, or the well-written,

objective editorial coverage? To illustrate the point, let me give an example, this time as a consumer rather than an active player in the PR game.

I recently contacted a building society after I had read in the money pages of the *Independent* that it was offering a particularly good interest rate. The article that caught my eye was all about how investors could take advantage of high interest rates; not just be crippled by them. An analysis pointed out which was the best performer currently available, and kindly gave a contact phone number at the end of the piece.

When I rang the building society concerned (no names, no pack drill!), the woman dealing with my enquiry sensibly asked where I had heard about the limited issue offer. I told her that I had read an article mentioning the offer in the *Independent*. 'But we're not going to advertise in the *Independent* until next week,' she said, 'so you must have seen a write-up.' She was right, of course. And when I asked her about people's reaction to the article, she had the number of calls generated by it at her fingertips.

Advertising checklist

So, you can see that there are no hard and fast rules on the advertising question. You really do have to use common sense to guide you. Before you agree to an ad, ask yourself these questions:

1. Has the newspaper/magazine already been supportive editorially? *Disregard* any promises of increased editorial support made during negotiations with the advertising department; consider the track record.
2. Will the salesperson give you at least a 10 per cent discount on the rate card? (Remember, the publication doesn't keep the cash; it normally goes to the advertising agency that placed the ad on behalf of the client. If you are dealing direct, why shouldn't you have the commission instead, but in discount form?)
3. How will you be able to appraise the impact of the ad?

Lastly, don't forget targeting. Is the readership profile 'right' for you? Remember, this is not a free plug via a press release. You are actually paying, so you want value for money.

Appraising the impact of your ad

Impact by postal response
Some magazines include free 'enquiry' cards, which are postage paid. The system works like this: if a reader is interested in your ad or editorial, he or she can tear out one of the pre-paid reply cards at the back of the magazine, which are number coded to match the contents. The reader then sends it back to the magazine, who in turn will pass the enquiries on to you, providing valuable feedback.

Impact by telephone response
Alternatively, if there is no enquiry card system, can you include a dedicated phone number, for potential punters to contact you direct? In this way, you can trace all enquiries on that particular line to your ad. If you don't have a spare phone line, you could include your usual number with the name of a specific individual as the contact. Obviously, if you get some calls asking for that person (and assuming you brief the person beforehand, of course!) you can then tell roughly how many callers are probably responding to your ad. This fact is worth knowing, especially as the sales rep will probably be on the phone again within three months, asking if you would like to support the magazine again.

Advertising on radio and TV

Independent radio stations (and, to a lesser extent, TV companies) will also be interested in talking to you about advertising. In the latter case, they may regard you as too small to deal with individually and so the enquiry may be no more than: 'Which is your advertising agency?'

When you have a budget in mind, radio may be well worth entertaining. Think about the sort of audience in the area and find out what kind of package the radio station will offer you. In many cases, the station will take on board the actual production of the ad free of charge as part of the package. The station may agree to sell you a series of ads which will go out over an agreed period. Media Expenditure Analysis Ltd estimates that over 20 per cent of ILR advertising is from local advertisers, according to Radio Marketing Bureau statistics.

Sometimes the package is impressive. Particularly good value for the smaller advertiser on radio is the current trend of 'splitting' (ie, the same radio station using two or more different frequencies to broadcast different material to different listeners). Quite often, this is in the form of an FM and an AM output, aiming for different age groups but sharing the original geographical area, which is dictated largely by the power of the transmitter and the Independent Broadcasting Authority (IBA).

In Chapter 6, we will consider how your PR efforts can work on radio without your spending a penny; that said, don't rule out advertising on your ILR station. You will probably find that you can get a better price by simply threatening to use the local newspaper for advertising instead! Interestingly, TV is not in this league of competition; budgets are normally much greater for a television campaign than for something over a similar period on radio and in local newspapers. But, once again, your skills at generating decent exposure will work equally well with TV news rooms as with anybody else, even if your budget is non-existent.

Check your approach

Lastly, as a footnote, try to get into a different frame of mind when you are dealing with the paid-for side. One day you might be talking to the news editor at your local paper, giving him a taster of this interesting story you have come across. The key word here is *giving*; this is not a transaction or a business deal and you should not mention money or advertising (unless it is strictly relevant to your story, as in the case of, say, an overseas contract).

The next day, however, you may need to ring the advertising department, and you should do so with a totally different attitude. There is no way you are 'giving' anything away; you want to do a deal on a space and you are going to do a good one.

This may sound like something approaching schizophrenia, but you will be surprised how easy it becomes. Media sales reps are hungry to get your cash out of you; they are often commission oriented and keen to close the deal. Journalists want good, interesting stories. If you're not providing one or the other you're probably wasting your breath.

CHAPTER 5
Words and Pictures

The importance of pictures

Just like love and marriage, words and pictures go together naturally, especially when you are thinking about ways to make an impact in the media. It doesn't matter if you are the world's worst photographer yourself; the important thing is that you learn to recognise the *potential* for pictures. Whenever serious photography is called for, I have always left it to the experts. Let the professionals worry about the light meters and the F stops (whatever they are). Your job as a promotions person is to offer the photographer the right subject to point at. If you've got that bit right, the photographer can handle it from there.

No press release should be drafted without at least asking: 'Is there a picture opportunity with this story?' If, when you are jotting down your first ideas, your answer to this is yes, then you are in a position to greatly enhance your chances of winning coverage. On the other hand, if the answer is no, you have lost nothing by asking the question; you can still meet your primary objective of passing on a good story to a journalist for editorial consideration.

A moment or two spent thinking about pictures will pay dividends. In some cases, a good idea for a 'picture' (for some reason, newspaper people avoid the expression 'photo') can actually work better in terms of securing column inches for your organisation than a press release, no matter how eloquently penned it may be. This is because a picture could catch the picture editor's eye in a way that your story in isolation might not.

All your media 'customers', with the obvious exception of radio journalists, have at least a passing interest in generating interesting visual images for their audience or readership. And, just as your press releases are designed to save news editors and reporters too much unnecessary legwork, you should also consider the needs of their colleagues, the picture editors. How can you provide them with an interesting shot?

Some journalists you deal with will regard pictures as a priority, at least equal to the actual content of the story under consideration. A friend who recently made the move from the written word into television production summed this up nicely: 'I don't care what the story is. My first question is always "What are the pictures?"' he said. In other words, as a television producer putting together a news and features package every night, there's more to the job than simply getting people in the studio to tell vivid stories. He depends on visually *interesting* material to punctuate the chunks of the show handled by the presenters and studio guests. Or, to put it bluntly, without the pictures, the show cannot go on. The most attractive news-reader (no matter how attractive) will start to bore viewers after a few minutes if all they see is somebody reading the autocue straight to camera. And, as an exercise in successful television, the production will have failed. People will switch off in their thousands.

In this chapter, we consider how pictures are relevant not just to TV, but also to local newspapers, national newspapers and the trade press. We will also touch on how your idea for a picture, if successfully managed, will carry across your key message in a way that a press release alone can never do. On the practical side, we will outline a little of the technical know-how you need to produce pictures to the right specification. But don't be put off; all you *really* require is the ability to arrange things for the professional photographer who you will be dealing with. That said, if you are a bit handy in the dark-room, you may be able to save yourself some cash when it comes to producing your own PR prints for issue to the printed press, and we will also see what those requirements might be.

Television

Moving pictures are not the only option available to those journalists working in television, but they are by far the most important. Granted, studio graphics (moving and static) are used to good effect, as are still pictures, although these are normally confined to 'portraits' of people in the news. The last time I saw a still landscape on the box it was used for the weather forecast. So, there is no getting away from it: what makes TV so very watchable is the moving image. That's why the main fall-back is often 'library' pictures, used to illustrate news stories put together at very short notice.

When you are dealing with your local TV station, bear this in mind. Don't offer a story which is one shot only. Try instead to think of a 'package' (ie, a series of related ideas, at least some of which are visually interesting). Jot down a few ideas and have them close to hand when you ring in the story. A sensible tip is to make picture notes in the margin of a copy of your press release. Nobody, but nobody, can escape the need for moving pictures; even politicians are asked to play the 'animation game' when they deal with TV crews. How often on TV have you seen somebody walking past the Houses of Parliament, apparently unaware of the camera, only to cut immediately to the interview? What the reporter has done is to ask the interviewee to act as a moving image, so that a 'voice-over' can be put on top of the picture by way of a narration or introduction. It may be contrived, but nobody seems to mind, especially the politicians.

The political interview is about as dry as television gets, visually speaking. You will stand a much higher chance of getting a TV crew to come to you if you have an interesting moving picture which you can offer to the news editor. (We will only consider roving or mobile camera crews in this section; studio/ personal appearances are covered in detail in Chapter 6.)

By way of an example, I once put together a package for a local TV news programme set in a gymnasium. The story was about how a business consultant had developed a 'fitness test' for management; the consultant had identified a new market for the gym – fat business executives – and trade was booming as a result. The coverage that resulted went something like this:

Image	Voice-over
1. Shot of chubby-ish business man at his desk, telling his secretary that he is going out to lunch.	Introduction
2. Shot of business man walking past pub.	Explanation
3. Shot of business man entering health club (external)	Explanation
4. Shot of business man changed and doing a work-out to 'body-popping' music.	Explanation
5. Interview with business man.	No voice-over
6. More work-out shots as reporter introduces consultant.	Link
7. Consultant explains scheme.	No voice-over
8. Gym coach talks about business.	No voice-over
9. More work-out shots.	Conclusion

The piece actually worked out to about four minutes of air time, but the package took nearly two hours to film! However, you can see that *each* of the nine stages has something visually interesting to offer the viewer. And intercutting/editing means that nobody can get bored with the same visual image for too long.

Quite what will appeal to the TV news editor/producer of the day is a tricky question. However, you will need to offer something approaching the example given to make your story attractive. As a bare minimum, you should have *two* elements for the TV crew to work with:

1. A subject who can be interviewed.
2. A visually interesting (probably animated) backdrop.

Your interviewee will probably be asked to do a 'two-shot' when the interview is finished. This means that the crew films your spokesperson doing no more than nodding and smiling; the footage is edited later to feed in the reporter's more interesting questions. This curious ritual is fairly common practice, as it avoids the need for two crews to cover each interview.

If you can't manage a moving backdrop, then arrange to do your interview in front of your logo; for example, if you are a retailer, outside your shop so your sign is in shot, or if you are a teacher or a school governor, have the school board behind you.

While on the subject of visiting TV crews, if your new whatever-it-is has the potential to fail, then you are asking for trouble inviting your local TV station to film it working. The funniest example I ever came across involved a company which claimed to have invented a device to stop reversing lorries accidently damaging parked vehicles that were in the driver's 'blind spot'. Lovely idea, and good pictures, so the local station jumped at it. The facility was all set up for the TV crew, complete with the device fitted to a lorry and the advertising executive's car parked in a suitably protruding way. The lorry reversed towards the car and, yes, you've guessed it, failed to stop. And all the time, the cameras kept rolling. That evening, when the station showed the incident on the evening news, I don't know who was the most upset – the advertising executive with the damaged motor or the so-called PR man who shot himself in the corporate foot so effectively. If only he'd checked the thing actually worked!

Subjects/news stories that will merit a mention on local TV are covered in Chapter 7. Actually drawing the crew to cover your facility is not so easy. As a general rule, however, typical magazine/regional news programmes will often favour a story which shows shots of people *doing* things as opposed to just *talking* about things. Pressure groups are the arch-exponents of this; the people waving placards outside the town hall are a lot more interesting visually than the people holding reasoned discussions inside. If you are a manufacturer, offer shots of people making things. If you have a new computer, show somebody working it. If you are promoting your school, then pupils acting in a play or active in a science lab are probably better 'pictures' than a boring classroom shot alone.

TV facility checklist

The following checklist may be useful when you are planning to lay on a 'facility' for the local TV crew:

1. What 'moving' pictures can you offer? (Animation, not emotion!)
2. Will the TV crew have access to at least one interviewee?
3. Can you arrange the facility for mid-morning, say 11 am? (This is considered to be the optimum time. An 11 am start means that you might get a second bite of the cherry, as, thanks to the speedy electronic news-gathering (ENG) process, your story could be filmed and edited ready to appear on the lunch-time local news as well as the magazine programme in the evening.)
4. Can you make the arrangements to accommodate (internal) disappointment? (We have already seen how PR options are sometimes hostage to other news stories; more than once I have laid on a facility only to cancel it because the TV crew have been diverted on the way to another job! Such a predicament can leave you with an internal problem. Despite what people say, they usually like the idea of appearing 'on the telly'. If you have raised their expectations and the crew has failed to appear, you will need a good reason up your sleeve! Also, remember that, although attracting the crew is good, it is not an automatic guarantee of coverage: the news editor may push your report out in favour of something more topical, for example.)
5. If you are offering to demonstrate a new machine/vehicle/ piece of technical apparatus, can you *depend* on it performing?

Local newspapers

Pictures are also important to your local newspaper. Have a look at one and see how many pages don't have at least one picture. General convention means that newspaper picture editors tend to follow the philosophy of Lewis Carroll's Alice in Wonderland: 'What is the use of a book,' thought Alice, 'without pictures or conversations?'

For design purposes, a picture breaks up a page of solid newspaper text, which can be unattractive. Some pictures are an integral part of the stories chosen (hence the need to think of pictures and press releases together) while others are there purely for their photogenic appeal, with perhaps a picture caption underneath to briefly set the scene with a few token words.

Things are changing on local newspapers. These days, thanks to new technology lowering production/printing costs, it's not at all uncommon to see a splash of colour on the front or back page.

Types of picture

For your purposes, there are three ways in which local newspapers acquire their pictures:

1. They are commissioned internally by the news desk (to illustrate a story).
2. They are provided 'on spec' by the staff photographer or a freelance photographer, both of whom have an eye for a nice shot and are successful in getting their work in.
3. They are submitted by people handling their own publicity as a free contribution to the newspaper for reproduction (probably to complement a press release).

TV and film pages are typically full of examples from the last category; they can also feature heavily in both news and features, depending, of course, on what else is available.

Taking the three approaches one by one, let's first think about the mechanics behind the news room commission.

Commissioned pictures

A reporter has a story involving somebody who does not normally feature in the newspaper, or even somebody who does, like a local politician, who is prepared to pose for the cameras doing something unusual. The reporter sends a note to the picture desk/photographic section requesting the sort of shot that is required. (This request is normally worded in a suitably diplomatic way; not many reporters would be brave enough to dare to tell a photographer how to do his or her job!) The photographer then makes the arrangements with the subject direct, attends and shoots – it's as simple as that.

If you are confident that your story has picture potential, the reporter dealing with your press release will probably set this

Above   Illustration from a book of games promoting Courvoisier. It accompanied a press release sent to a monthly magazine. *Photographer* Patrick Lichfield.

Overleaf   Equipment is more interesting when it is shown in use. A good promotional picture can make a kitchen sink very desirable.

chain of events in motion. You need to do no more than perhaps lay on a facility for the photographer when he or she calls.

'On spec' pictures

This sort of picture is 'snapped' by staff photographers while doing the 'rounds'; something appeals to the artist within, and the photographer acts on spec, investing a little of his or her time with some of the newspaper's film to provide a nice shot. Such shots can be of anything and everything – perhaps topical, but not necessarily.

Submitted pictures

This third category is of most use to you. Local newspapers being as busy as they are, it may be that the photographer has difficulty doing all the jobs that are available – what with hard news stories to take on board as well. Fires and floods wait for no man, and they will probably take first call on the news photographer's time. So, a publicist will tend to cut out the middle man (ie, the busy photographer) and send in a picture to the editor direct, in a format that will be of immediate use to the publication (ie, black and white, glossy and normally about 10 by 8 inches).

Here are two examples of submitted pictures, sent to a weekly newspaper on spec. The first is from Le Bureau du Cognac Courvoisier, illustrating one of the games in a new book called *As the Meal Ended*, which is itself a vehicle for promoting the Courvoisier product. Depending on the eventual reproduction size, the Courvoisier name could appear twice: once on the bottle on the table and once on the matchbox!

The second example is from the Metal Sink Manufacturers' Association. Sensibly, the product is illustrated in use, and is not just a boring shot of a sink standing alone.

The same composition rules apply as for television pictures: active rather than passive subjects and with a person in the picture rather than, say, just a product. By the way, do not go down the road of gratuitous sexism; pictures of your new lathe gain nothing by having a topless woman draped across it. Not only are such shots offensive, they are also unlikely to appeal to the editor of a family newspaper with a general readership. They are also faintly ridiculous.

Try to get your logo in the picture somehow – a poster on the office wall is better than nothing at all. Experts in corporate image refer to this as 'subliminal reinforcement', but in simple terms it means that you can't use your logo too much.

A good tip is to ask the local newspaper photographer if he or she is available for freelance work. Invariably, the photographer will agree to do a PR picture for you (the sort that will appeal to, say, the local newspaper), saving you the time and bother of briefing a local photographic studio. For some reason, the average high-street photographer is ill at ease with anything other than the studio environment, and so is unlikely to produce pictures with a suitably 'newsy' feel. However, this type of photographer may be helpful if you are producing a 'new faces' press release (see Chapter 3) and want to include a studio-type shot. (Some people still prefer to have the shot done in the workplace so they can get the organisation's logo in as well.)

You may decide that you can handle this type of picture yourself in-house; remember, you need glossy shots, either 10 by 8 or 8 by 6 inches. And don't ask for them back – you won't get them! Be prepared to speculate the pound or so that each print will cost you.

Perhaps one of the best tried and tested means of getting a picture into the local paper is the 'big cheque' shot. This is the simplest way of graphically illustrating somebody handing over a sum of cash to somebody else.

If you are giving a significant donation to a charity or a cash prize to a lucky winner, the shot is always the same: you or your representative on one side of the giant cheque, the grateful recipient on the other. Try to give your local bank plenty of notice if you wish to borrow a giant cheque. The Midland Bank is kind enough to provide this service free of charge, and you may find that the other three high-street giants follow suit. Needless to say, it's useful free publicity for the bank as well.

On a practical note, these big cheques come in a 'wipe-clean' format, so that you can fill in your own details before the presentation at the photocall. You will probably find that the bank will want the cheque back when you have finished with it, which is fair enough as they probably only have a limited number.

Try not to rely exclusively on 'big cheque' photocalls for your local paper: once every so often is OK, but offer other opportunities as well. Apart from anything else, the 'big cheque' syndrome is so widespread that it's becoming a little overworked. Freesheets in particular sometimes seem to publish little else! Nevertheless, the 'big cheque' is a good stand-by for when you have money to give away for whatever reason.

National newspapers

If you find something that is particularly photogenic in your organisation, then it could appeal to the picture desks of the national newspapers. Realistically, we are talking about the larger, 'heavy' titles, who can give a picture a decent spread across five or six columns. It is highly unlikely that the *Daily Mirror*, for example, would be interested in these two recent examples of the genre: an unusual breed of sheep, shot in their native Highlands (featured in the *Independent*), and a little girl playing with an unusual electric globe for sale at Hamleys (which made the front page of the *Guardian*).

Once again, these pictures are sometimes chosen by the photographer, but more often they are commissioned by the picture desk. The best way to contact the picture desk of a national newspaper is by phone, to see if the desk is interested in the shot, followed by a faxed note, giving details of when and where the job is. A straightforward memo-style note is all that is required, with brief details and a contact number for follow-up enquiries. You should aim to make contact two days before the event; and remember that you are appealing to a newspaper, so don't give the impression that the picture could be taken any time within the next six months. Use the topical 'hook' you have included in your press release as an entrée, then briefly explain the picture. As a rule of thumb, it is best to offer your 'picture call' (as it is known) to several papers, simply because it increases your chance of coverage.

If you succeed in getting one of the national photographers to your job, you have done well. Afford him or her every facility, but remember that the photographer is the expert, not you. Hand the photographer a copy of your press release before leaving the scene; it will provide caption material, or at least a contact point (your spokesman) for further information. The caption is run underneath the picture and is usually a minimum of two lines, which in typical broadsheet terms means about 35–40 words.

The picture may be used nationally, for a regional page or even for an early edition, pending something more newsy which pushes it out. If it hasn't appeared within about three days, ring the picture editor or the actual photographer (though the latter will probably be harder to reach) and ask for a steer as to timing. There is no guarantee that it will be used at all. But, on the other hand, don't be too disappointed if it doesn't appear the next day; your picture, if it will stand alone, could be held over for a suitable slot a day or so later. Either way, it's worth a call to check.

Trade press

Your stock black-and-white picture is also worth sending to your trade press; it could 'make' a useful inside picture, accompanied by a suitable press release. However, if you have something special to offer, you could do even better, and perhaps win a slot on the cover. But this will take some negotiation. The last thing you want to do is to arrange expensive colour photography on spec. First, contact the editor direct with what you have in mind. Offer a choice of format to suit the publication: it will almost certainly be a colour shot, but some editors prefer $2\frac{1}{4}$ inch transparencies to colour prints, as the former give better quality reproduction. It's worth discussing not only the format but also the deadline: When is the latest your picture should be on the editor's desk? Monthly magazines may be committed well in advance, so the timing question is important.

The editor will need to be convinced of two things before offering you valuable cover space: that the picture itself will be interesting to the readership (and potential readership, if the title is distributed by news stands) and that the quality of the picture will be good enough for reproduction. Even then, the editor may not be prepared to make a commitment. Bear in mind that the editor may also be under some pressure from advertising colleagues to let them 'sell' the cover to an advertiser, so he or she will need to satisfy him or herself that your picture is a good one, with plenty of appeal to the specialised readership.

Away from the front cover, your colour transparencies could win a valuable space as part of the centre spread. Your selection of shots should be thought of as part of a package to make this option work: first, three good shots (one to act as the main shot, with two smaller variations to provide additional interest), then the words – not just a press release, but a pukka article written in the style of the magazine. This should be on plain A4 paper, double spaced, and with a word count at the end. You should aim for around 1000 words, but be guided by the editor.

It's worth stressing again that the quality of interest will be critical. If the idea is wrong, then it won't make the 'spread'; the editor will use either a staff-written feature or a freelance contribution instead. Both of these will cost time and/or money, but in editorial terms it's cash well spent. Any editor worth his or her salt will insist on quality editorial, and not what has become known as 'PR puff'. The question is: Can you ensure the same quality without the expense? If so, the centre spread in a trade magazine could be yours for the asking.

A note on commissioning pictures

Bear in mind when you are commissioning pictures that you can easily achieve added value above and beyond your PR drive. Are you producing any literature? If so, professional transparencies will be better for your designer/printer to work with, and you will save yourself production costs if you have a small library of stock shots to draw on. In an ideal world, you would have similar material in all three formats ($2\frac{1}{4}$ inch transparency, colour print, and black-and-white print). The former will also be handy if you are producing any display material for exhibition stands. Ask your photographer to shoot colour negatives as well as black-

and-white ones – the cost of the extra film is minimal, and you
only have to call out the photographer once.

CHAPTER 6
Tackling Interviews

Preparation

First, the good news. If you can interest the media in interviewing you, the chances are you are going to shine. You want to talk to the reporter, and that reporter actually wants to talk to you. Not only that, it's in his or her interests to help you relax and to get you talking confidently – the more the better.

Now, the bad news. If you haven't prepared for an interview, then you are going to have one of the worst experiences of your life. You will hear yourself blurt out things you never meant to say. Your voice will crack and sound like somebody else's. For several minutes, you may feel physically sick. Afterwards, when the perspiration has stopped, the long-term worry will set in. Not only did you embarrass yourself in front of the reporter, but, now, thousands of people will see or hear the results of your indiscretions. Perhaps your boss will be among them, or one of your best customers, or your family. At best, you will feel that you didn't perform well and wish you hadn't got involved. And at worst, well, it could take you quite some time to live it down.

Are you worried yet? I hope so, because here comes a golden rule: before you open your mouth, *prepare*.

Whether it's an interview with the press, local radio or national TV, the preparation rule applies. You owe it to yourself, and your organisation, to ensure that you are ready for each performance. To give you a general framework, you must cover these three aspects during your preparation:

1. Content

2. Key message
3. Technique.

If you agree to do an interview and you are not confident in all three areas, you are courting danger. In Chapter 9, we will talk about how you may find yourself acting as spokesperson under less than perfect conditions, perhaps during a crisis.

The point here is that, even when you have successfully created your own opportunities through well-constructed press releases, there is still no room for complacency. Without preparation, you may end up with that most unhappy result in the PR game – the own goal. The reason is simple. Any interview effectively moves you away from the considerable control you enjoyed with a press release. Before, if you wanted to search for the *bon mot*, there was no problem; you could set aside your draft press release and indulge yourself, bringing the fruits of your labour back to the typewriter with you. This is *not* the case in an interview. For one thing, it is hard to misquote a press release, but it is not at all hard when you are talking to somebody who isn't sure what he or she wants to say. And if you don't know quite how to express yourself quickly and effectively, the time to find out is during your preparation, not when you are face to face with the interviewer.

Clearly, if you have put together your press release from scratch, you will already have a fair idea of the content of the story you are offering. When the newspaper wants to talk to you further, or the radio station asks you into the studio, you are already on familiar ground subjectwise. Even if you are satisfied that you know your stuff – the *content* element – resist the temptation to give a firm yes until you are equally sure of both your *key message* and the *technique* you will adopt for the interview. No reporter will mind if you say you are tied up right now, but you promise to ring back in five minutes. However, try not to leave it longer than five minutes. Bear in mind that you are not the only person in the world the reporter wants to talk to. And ring back even if you decide against accepting the interview offer; it's only polite really, and you will avoid being accused of mucking the reporter around when he or she is working against deadlines.

We covered the importance of key messages in press releases in Chapter 2. They are all the more critical when you find yourself doing that first interview.

Finally, a health warning: if you suffer from undue shyness, no amount of coaching is going to make you feel any better when you tackle a TV or radio interview. This is in contrast to nervousness, which is a perfectly understandable by-product when you are performing an unusual task and you want to do well. So, let preparation be your solution to anxiety, but if you don't want to get involved with interviews because you feel temperamentally unsuited, that's fine, too. Only you can decide.

No matter how introvert or extrovert you may be, you should still take advantage of the advice given in the following section on press interviews; even if you don't relish the prospect, you should look through the sections on radio and television interviews as well. But don't feel that you have to run the electronic media gauntlet if you don't want to. Perhaps there is somebody else in your organisation who can step in once you have set up the interview. Or if push comes to shove, you will have to decline, saying simply: 'You've already got the press release – do what you like with it.' Personally, I don't think this is the best way forward; generally speaking, the opportunities to shine outweigh the possible calamities, provided whoever you field to perform the interview does his or her homework beforehand.

After I once quoted a client in a press release, the local independent radio station rang me to ask me to rig up an interview with him. He knew his stuff all right, but I still tried to get him out of it, for the simple reason that he had the most awful stammer. Not only that, but I knew from watching him work that the more nervous he became, the worst the stammer got! Desperately, I sought a substitute, but in vain. The deadline meant that the substitute I had mentally earmarked was unavailable. So, we ended up doing the interview, which was a mistake. The reporter's tape was almost unusable as it required so much fine editing. Bear this unhappy tale in mind when we look at radio and television interviewing techniques, but, first, the written press.

Press interviews

Here is the background: assuming your story is strong enough, you may be asked to do a press interview, based on or inspired by your own press release.

This is excellent; you have created an opportunity from scratch to deliver your key message in person, filling in the gaps that have been left by your press release and putting a human touch to the story. The most likely situation is that a journalist will ring you, having been passed your press release to work on by the news editor of the paper or magazine. Don't be offended if the journalist has some additional queries; no matter how well constructed your press release is, there may be aspects of the story that the journalist wants to clarify or highlight. Be as helpful as you can on the phone and ring the journalist back as soon as you are able if you can't deal with the enquiry there and then.

On-the-record only

That telephone interview may be all that is required by the journalist, or it could be a request to meet you and interview you face to face, perhaps with a photographer on hand. Either way, treat this initial contact as *on-the-record*. There is no need for either of you to state this; all conversations with journalists are assumed to be on-the-record (ie, for quotation and possible direct attribution to you personally). In other words, everything you tell the journalist could be written down and used against you, so be friendly and frank, but don't go beyond your remit at this stage. Keep a copy of your press release beside you during the phone interview.

I'm not saying that journalists set out to deliberately misquote their interviewees, or get them into trouble by betraying a confidence, but it does happen occasionally. If you keep your answers as factual and straightforward as possible, you will cut the risk considerably. If the journalist wants to meet you for an interview, that's better still, although time pressures often mean that a few questions on the phone are the easiest supplement to your press release. If you do arrange a meeting, the journalist may ask to tape the interview. This seems to be common practice in these days of reliance on gadgets (whatever happened to shorthand?) so don't be inhibited. A good technique is to have your own tape recorder handy; when the journalist produces his or hers, you can produce yours – that way, everybody's happy!

In Chapter 8, we will look at the advantages of going off-the-record, as well as the dangers that go with it. But for primary contact with journalists, on-the-record is the safest option by far, especially when you are dealing with your own stories and not theirs.

On a practical note, you can encourage a journalist to do a feature on your organisation by involving him or her directly. If you run a flying school, for example, offer to take the journalist and a photographer up with you so they can experience it for themselves. The same goes for any 'activity' story your organisation can offer, especially if you are involved with teaching. Bear in mind that if a journalist takes the time and trouble to follow up your press release, the chances are that he or she wants to find out more about your set-up, which can only be good.

There is no guarantee that the journalist will automatically write a favourable piece, and there is a chance that you could be, not to put too fine a point on it, stitched up. However, it is more likely that *you* will let yourself down during the interview, by making an off-hand remark or joke which then lands you in the mire when you actually see the piece in print. Remember, *everything* you say is fair game, so the onus is on you to say only the things that you want to say. The famous story about President Ronald Reagan saying 'We are about to start bombing the Russians', which got world-wide coverage, was apparently no more than a voice test for the microphone before a press conference started. So, save the wisecracks until your interview with the press is over, or you will run the risk of seeing them taken out of context.

Follow-up

Assuming that the interview goes well, remember to ask when the piece will appear. You may need extra copies for your friends/clients, but don't expect the journalist to provide these for you.

Another useful tip is to give the journalist a ring as soon as he or she gets back to the office. There are two reasons for this: first, it's polite to say thank you for taking the time and interest to come and talk to you; second, there may be one or two things that have occurred to the journalist on the way back to the office. With the best will in the world, these may slip the journalist's mind, especially if, on returning to the office, the journalist finds his or her desk covered with messages and other things that need immediate attention. So, if *you* ring the journalist, you give him or her the opportunity to ask you those forgotten questions.

A final thought
Have a copy of your press release available to give to the journalist before he or she leaves. Any complex statistics/figures that are needed to make your point should also be on paper to save possible confusion when the journalist actually sits down to write the piece.

Radio interviews

Format
If a radio station news room picks up on your press release, the interview that follows will be in one of these four formats:

1. Down the line (on the telephone, taped or live).
2. Taped by the reporter during the visit.
3. Taped by the reporter at the studio.
4. Live at the studio.

The choice depends on a number of factors, including your availability, deadline pressures and the format of the show that the interview is meant for. The *Today* programme on BBC Radio 4 uses all four variations, which apart from anything else provides a good contrast for the listener. Stories that lend themselves to 'actuality' (the sound of something other than the human voice) often involve a visit from the reporter with a portable tape recorder. However, tight budgets and deadlines tend to push the smaller local radio stations away from interviews out of the office. A duty reporter can cover a lot more stories by staying close to the studio and using methods 1, 3 and 4 than by going out on every story.

If you do have a choice when the station first contacts you, try to persuade the reporter that it is worth making the journey. The story will, to a large extent, determine your chances of success; a straightforward appointment story can be done quickly and effectively either down the line or in the studio, without deploying a reporter. A story involving interesting noises, on the other hand, stands a much better chance of a visit because of the nature of the medium. Anything from a swimming pool to a concert hall, a hen house to a race-track is good; they are all likely to catch the news editor's ear and the radio reporter's imagination.

The nice thing about recording your first interview on your premises and not theirs is that you will feel more at ease. The tape recorder that the reporter will bring is certainly not as intimidating as the studio mike. It's probably a good idea to tell the reporter if you have never done a recorded interview before.

Preparation

You should suggest that you discuss the story and plan a broad outline for the interview before the recorder is turned on. The reporter will probably welcome this idea as well; the chances are that he or she has not really had a chance to read your press release in any detail, so he or she will appreciate a chance to spend a minute or two thinking about the subject.

When you are both happy, the interview proper can begin. The reporter will probably sit fairly close to you to ensure that the mike picks up enough of your voice for sound level purposes. The first question is normally a double-check. A very popular opening shot is 'What did you have for breakfast today?' followed by 'What is your name and full title?' The former is to ensure that your voice is loud enough to be picked up from where you are sitting, whereas the latter will help back at the studio to identify the speaker on tape.

Another technique widely used by radio reporters is the 'dumped' first question. This is usually about something related to the story; an unimportant detail which may or may not be included – not the sort of thing you would have included in the intro to your press release. This question is to make you feel at ease with the interview and to get you over any initial nervousness. It isn't really meant for the final piece and will probably be edited out back at the studio, but bear in mind what happened to Ronald Reagan!

The SMOK rule

For all radio interviews, live or recorded, down the line or in the studio, I have devised the SMOK rule:

S   *Smile!* Surprisingly, it will show in your voice and you will sound brighter and better.

M   *Modulate.* Move your voice up and down in pitch to avoid monotony, which is a major turn-off in radio terms. The reporter will do it during the questions – follow his or her example!

O   *Open up.* Use personal instances to illustrate your points: 'The other day one of my customers asked me that question. . . .' And give your story a human dimension wherever possible. Don't say: 'Eighty per cent of the company's target market.' Say instead: 'Eight out of ten of my customers.'

K   *Key messages.* Have three or four jotted down on the press release in front of you for easy reference.

Your key message

As soon as you feel the interview is under way, start to use your key messages to make your point. The whole interview may only last four minutes, so don't leave it too long!

I have been an observer at several radio training courses, and, more than once, the students have expressed disappointment after their interview exercise. They complained that they didn't get a chance to weave their key message in. When asked about it afterwards, they said that the reporter kept asking the wrong questions.

So, here is the hub of the successful radio interview: never mind the question, just give the answer you want to (the best key message), and make it relevant. For this approach to work, you must effectively take control of the interview. Your checklist of key messages is as relevant to the interview as the reporter's key questions, after all. And remember, you are *not* passive in the interview process; without you there would be no interview! Don't be intimidated by the mike; tell yourself that the reporter's questions are no more important than your answers. Watch a few politicians being interviewed and you will see what I mean. They are the experts at this technique, and any good journalist will be wise to this. For example, Sir Robin Day once asked Margaret Thatcher: 'Prime Minister, what will be your answer to my first question?'

Your key messages will be your 'lifebelt' during the interview. They mean you won't be stuck for an answer, no matter how awkward or ungainly the question may be. As you start to give one of your key messages in response to a question, the interview will flow and you will feel more and more in control. The following example illustrates these points:

Your story:

Fewer men than ever are wearing hats, according to your company, Newtown Hats, who carried out a recent survey.

Your key messages:

- The best dressed men still wear hats.
- Newtown Hats also stocks quality hats for women, now selling better than ever.
- Newtown Hats has the widest range of fashion accessories in the High Street/oldest established millinery shop.
- Opening a new branch in Oldtown in the new year to meet business demand.

Extract from local radio interview:

Reporter: Can you tell me your full name and position please? (fiddling with tape recorder)

You: I am Jack McVitie, owner of Newtown Hats in the High Street.

Reporter: A recent survey has shown that fewer men than ever before are wearing hats these days. Why do you think this is?

You: Well, we have been selling hats in Newtown for 30 years now, and our sales of men's hats has never been lower. Our survey showed that eight out of ten male customers just don't feel comfortable in hats any more – certainly not for everyday wear.

Reporter: You say not for everyday wear. Do you find there is still a demand for special occasions then?

You: That's right. Top hats for weddings are a very popular line, and we have found that really fashion-conscious men still like to have access to a range of quality hats, especially if they are putting on the style!

Reporter: Well, surely you must be going out of business if all you do is sell something that nobody seems to need these days? Don't you feel a bit like a dinosaur?

You: Actually, that's not the case at all. Our sales of quality women's hats have never been better. The sort of lady who comes into our High Street branch knows exactly what she is looking for, and we always have a wide stock for her to choose from. And there's all our other fashion accessories like scarves and gloves.

Reporter: But surely, if there is no longer the demand, as the survey shows, won't you just drop men's hats entirely?

You: No, that's not the plan, not for the Newtown branch, or our Oldtown branch which opens next year. You see, my father, who started Newtown Hats back in the fifties, always used to say that we should aim to keep every customer happy, irrespective of whether they just wanted a cloth cap or a topper to get married in.

And you never know when there is going to be a sudden upturn in trade.

Reporter: That's not likely, surely? (laughing)

You: Well, I think you'd be surprised. Last year, every black pork-pie hat in the shop was sold out within a week. We couldn't get enough of them. (smiling)

Reporter: Why was that?

You: Well, the local polytechnic was holding a Blues Brothers party ... so everybody needed a pork-pie hat to wear. We also sold a lot of sun-glasses as well ....

Studio interview checklist
Here are some other pointers for a studio interview:

1. Present your business card so they know exactly who you are when you arrive. You may laugh, but people have been known to go to the wrong studio and face the wrong interviewer!
2. Take your own mini tape recorder. You can then listen to and evaluate your performance afterwards. If yours is a live interview, there won't be a copy unless you have asked somebody to tape it when you go on air. And even if it's a taped/edited interview, you will have to try to get a copy of the tape out of the station. Best to have your own copy.
3. Live interviews. There won't be as much time for you or the reporter to chat around the subject. Go straight into your key messages as soon as possible. Make sure that you can slot your phone number into the interview – learn it off by heart – and give the presenter a copy afterwards so he or she can repeat it. He or she can only say no!
4. The sizzle, not the steak. Don't *ever* get bogged down in minutiae; state simply what your new widget will do to make life easier – not the boring details about precisely how the thing works. Save those for the trade/technical press!
5. Impose your will. The reporter/presenter can only know very little about your subject area, so don't let him or her dominate

the interview. If in doubt about anything, just stop talking. This is better than saying something you will regret later. If the pause is awkward, it's not your problem, it's the presenter's. The presenter has to fill the airspace, not you. If you simply shut up after giving a satisfactory answer, the presenter will have to change tack or risk losing the flow of the interview.

6. Check the conditions out. Ask (before the interview starts) what the first question will be. Also, check if anybody else is being interviewed, or only you. You could be part of a gladiatorial type of entertainment, with you versus a rival firm/pressure group. I'm not saying refuse automatically, but it's better to know in advance!

Television interviews

Television interviews are probably the most important interviews that you will ever perform, certainly in terms of the size of the audience. Network programmes aside, even an early evening regional magazine show such as the BBC's *Newsroom South East* will offer you something in the region of two million viewers at the right time of year. This is about four times the circulation of the *Evening Standard*, which covers broadly the same area (London/South East). Although London-based Capital Radio claims an 'impact value' of four-fifths that of television, you must remember that Capital is far from typical. Apart from anything else, it is the largest ILR station in Britain.

Audience figures are one thing. How you make an impression on them is something else. The TV interview presents you with your greatest opportunity to perform well and to create a good impression. But there is a down side; television interviews carry considerable pressure and can be very stressful. Press and radio interviews are comparatively relaxed when set against the alien atmosphere of the TV studio. And once again, your performance will depend to a large extent on your preparation beforehand; if anything, being confident of both your material and your technique is more important for TV than either the print media or radio.

Young people listen to the radio and grown-ups read newspapers, but *everybody* watches television. Well, not quite everybody. Recent government statistics indicate that 2 per cent of UK households don't have a television set.

Before you accept . . .
So, where does this leave you when the local TV station contacts you to do an interview? With any luck, you already know why the station is ringing you; if you have offered a good treatment through a press release (see Chapter 3), your story could provide the basis for a recorded piece to be inserted into the evening news/magazine show. If this is the case, the station is probably contacting you to arrange a filming facility, so well done. But don't assume that this is the only reason the station has contacted you – you've got some important checks to do first.

For the sake of the following discussion, let's imagine that the TV station wants you to go into the studio to do a live interview, and your first at that.

While still on the phone, try to glean as much information as possible about this opportunity, which could be a valuable one. Tell whoever has contacted you that your organisation may be able to provide a spokesperson to go into the studio but that you need to jot down a few details and ring them back with an answer. It doesn't matter if it's you or a colleague who eventually ends up baking under the studio lights; you need as much information as possible at this stage to help you to decide. For example, get an idea of the subject matter of the programme and assess the general line of questioning. In this way, you will be able to gather your best material and work out your key messages to match it. Make your own checklist, including those elements given in the checklist here, so that you have as much background as possible. Even if the researcher cannot answer every question, because he or she doesn't know, you will still have a fair idea of what exactly you are taking on.

In television, nothing is carved in stone; things change all the time. So, remember to confirm the details of the interview when you arrive at the studio; you may find that, since you accepted the offer at 10 o'clock this morning, a news story has developed which you know nothing about. You couldn't be expected to know, but the story may have changed the priorities. The producer may now have different ideas about how to conduct your interview but has forgotten to tell you. The onus is, once again, on *you* to do a final check. If things have changed, don't accuse the people concerned of deliberately moving the goalposts; it could be that subsequent events have changed their original ideas.

TV interview checklist

1. Who is the interview request from (name of producer/researcher)?
2. What is the station?
3. What is the telephone number?
4. What is the name of the programme?
5. How long will the programme last? The interview?
6. When will the programme be broadcast (date/time)?
7. What is the subject matter?
8. Why exactly do they want you?
9. Who else will be taking part, if anyone?
10. What type of interview will it be?
    Live?
    Recorded as live?
    Recorded for later editing?
    Studio, one to one?
    Studio, debate style?
    Remote (unmanned) studio?
11. What style of programme will it be?
    Interview?
    Interview plus film?
12. What is the intended audience (rough viewing figures)?
13. Where will the interview take place (location)? Is there an alternative location?
14. At what time will the interview take place?
15. Who will be the interviewer/presenter?
16. What will be the line of questioning?
17. When do they need to know by?

Remember, check the details again when you arrive at the studio, because things change quickly.

Preparing your case: an example scenario

Imagine that you run a small independent garage-cum-filling station and you are about to set off around the world in a car to raise cash for charity. Good, human interest stuff. Seeing the PR potential, you have done a press release and sent all the local media outlets a picture of you and your co-driver beside the car, maps unfurled, planning your route. Coverage has already been pleasing, with picture stories in the evening and weekly paper. And this morning, the regional TV station rang to ask you to appear on the evening show. However, the researcher on the line says that she doesn't want your co-driver; just you on your own.

Great, you think, another opportunity to talk about the Newtown Garage round-the-world sponsorship. But as you start to fill in your TV interview checklist, a different story emerges. The researcher talks in vague terms about 'the motor trade and the environment' and the importance of businesses like your garage in the Newtown community.

Working your way down the list, it gradually dawns on you that the TV news room is not so much interested in your round-the-world sponsorship as the controversial plan to use part of the field at the back of your garage for a new workshop. You recall how a very vocal group of conservationists objected strongly when you applied for planning permission, but were overruled at a Newtown District Council planning committee meeting last week. There was a short piece about it in the local weekly paper, the *Newtown Gazette*, on Friday and today is Monday.

Assume that the researcher's non-committal answers have alerted you. She says something about the possibility of somebody going on 'with you'. Also, you are a bit puzzled by the fact that the researcher doesn't want to film you and the co-driver by the car (which would be the natural illustration for your story). This would also explain why she doesn't want your co-driver in the studio with you.

You will need to be armed with *two* sets of key messages: your positive points to make about the charity drive, and your positive points to make about your plans for the field at the back of your garage, just in case.

Jot down your six key messages (three to cover each story) and remember to keep them as simple as you can. These will form part of your SMOK preparation before you go to the studio.

Key messages
(Charity drive)

1. ....
....

2. ....
....

3. ....
....

(Workshop expansion into field)

1. ....
....

2. ....
....

3. ....
....

The points about the charity drive could be:

1. You want to support X, a local charity, because you believe the work it does is important (can you offer a personal instance?).
2. Adventure of a lifetime for you; nice to think somebody else will benefit.
3. People who wish to sponsor your charity drive (perhaps a pound per country) can drop in and sign up in reception at

Newtown Garage. (All sponsors are entered in a special prize draw and could win a week's free car hire from Newtown Garage.)

The points about the planning permission could be:

1. Glad you have had council approval for plans to build a new workshop so the garage business can expand.
2. Possible new jobs in time; new workshop means garage can stay at Newtown and not move away.
3. Environmental disruption will be kept to a minimum during building; rest of field will be undisturbed to preserve wildlife.

A possible slogan that you could keep up your sleeve is: 'How Green is my Garage'.

Before you go . . .
When you are happy with your key messages and you have agreed to appear, think about the following *before* you set off to the studio:

1. Can you tape the show?

A tape of your performance will be invaluable, not just for posterity, but also so you can learn from your mistakes. Set the video yourself, or make arrangements to get somebody to record it for you. (Again, don't rely on the TV station.)

2. Choosing your wardrobe.

How you look on television will determine how viewers see your organisation. While you don't want to look too formal, you should aim to project an image which is both relaxed and businesslike. For men, this really means a jacket and tie (leave the rally jacket at home for this one!) and avoid 'busy checks'; these can cause a distracting 'rippling' effect on the screen. If you suffer from rampant dandruff, then a light colour is better than black or navy blue; it will look smarter and you will feel better, knowing your scales aren't so obvious! Women should avoid loose, dangling ear-rings which can clatter and swing when you are making your points. Generally, go for light materials if possible;

the studio will be hot enough under all the lights and you want to stay as cool as you can, physically and mentally.

3. Do you really need glasses?

If you must wear glasses (and, ideally, you won't need them), ensure that they are not the 'Reactolite' kind, which go dark in sunlight. If they are, you could be heading for image problems; you will give the impression that you are wearing sun-glasses. (Nobody wants to see a member of the Cosa Nostra on their tea-time telly.) Not only does this look a bit affected in February, for example, but there is a serious psychological point here; if people can't see your eyes, you will not be communicating so effectively. Put bluntly, you will appear less 'trustworthy'. Just as somebody who avoids eye contact with you in conversation makes you wary, so viewers will feel slightly ill at ease subconsciously if they can't see your eyes.

4. No alcohol.

Do not be tempted to have a drink before you go on; even one can make its presence felt in a negative way. The heat of the studio tends to bring out the worst in people's noses, and if you start slurring as well, it's definitely bad news! You will need all your wits about you, so leave the drinking until you are in the hospitality suite afterwards. (There may be a carafe of water, which is useful. A sip before you start speaking will help you to stay cool and will calm your nerves.)

At the studio

The SMOK rule (Smile, Modulate, Open, Key message) applies to TV as much as to radio, although, to be realistic, you cannot smile all the time. If the subject you are discussing is serious, then, obviously, you don't want to sit there grinning inanely. Forcing a smile is difficult when you are nervous, so add this tip to your preparation list: think of something that makes you smile, like a punch line to a joke you have heard recently. When you need to smile, bring it to mind and this will make smiling much easier.

In reception, you will probably be met by one of the programme assistants or researchers, who will take you through to the studio area. Everybody will be very busy, running around with clipboards and making last minute checks before you go on air.

You may not get a chance to talk to the interviewer, but that doesn't matter (as long as you have checked with the producer/news editor that the line of questioning has not changed).

You will be seated on the set, where the temperature will already be beginning to rise under the lights. With luck, the production assistant (PA) will have automatically taken you via make-up. This is important, to get you into a 'performance' frame of mind. And if, like me, you are suffering from a distinct lack of hair, the make-up people will ensure that your pate won't dazzle anybody.

Use your time in the make-up chair constructively. Mentally run through your key messages/anecdotes again, without notes. Remember, you don't need gritty detail. It will slow down your flow and bore the viewers. Have no more than two statistics memorised, and for goodness sake don't try to refer to notes. If the make-up assistants are a chatty bunch, ask them what they think about the presenter: What is his or her style? Is he or she aggressive or reasonable? Does he or she ask short questions or long ones? Any advance intelligence you can get from this reliable source will be useful to you before the grilling starts!

After you have finished in make-up, I strongly recommend that you ask to use the loo. The next stop is the studio floor, and once you are in there, that's it. You'll have enough on your mind without worrying about what's in your bladder as well. When you do finally arrive on the studio floor, don't be surprised to find activity approaching fever pitch. Cameras will be moving across the floor, and people will be pulling cables, sticking on the last bits of the set and adjusting autocues (which are on the front of the cameras).

The floor manager or one of the technicians will probably attach a mini microphone to your shirt or blouse; these seem more popular these days than desk-top mikes. Now, for the first time, you will see your interviewer, and if anybody else is going to be on with you. This is where your hard work earlier in the day will pay off; you won't be surprised to find yourself sitting next to somebody who you know doesn't share many of your views!

The moment you are seated, start to relax consciously. Take long, deep breaths quietly and think about your posture. Here is a list of dos and don'ts to help you:

Don't:

- slump in the chair (looks sloppy/blasé);
- sit on the edge of the chair (looks nervous);
- clasp/wring your hands or bite your nails (also avoid licking your lips – most unattractive!).

Do:

- sit comfortably, resting against the back of the chair;
- use the arm rests and relax your hands in front of you (palms down, fingers still);
- cross your legs if it helps you, but not if it means you look too casual. For the sake of posture, try crossing your ankles instead.

Introduce yourself to the presenter/interviewer and remember to establish what the first question will be. When the 'on air' light goes on and the floor manager silently counts down from five, make sure that you keep your posture looking good; the first image you want to show the viewer is one of calm and confidence. A useful tip here is to spend some time concentrating on your blinking. Frequent blinking is a sure-fire give away that you are nervous or under pressure. If you can consciously keep your blinking to a minimum, and deliberately blink slowly when you do so, you will give an impression of somebody in control, and, in television terms, that first impression is all-important. Remember that the camera may be on you when the presenter introduces you, even if that is not the start of your interview. In other words, your impression – positive or negative – could be projected to the viewers before you even open your mouth. So smile!

On-screen conflict

If your interview is preceded by a filmed report with which you disagree, you will need to say so, politely but firmly, as soon as the questioning starts. Follow up immediately with the appropriate key message, and try to avoid getting drawn into a row about the film.

Likewise, if the programme has deliberately engineered a 'conflict' debate, with both the interviewer and your opponent trying to goad you, fight the temptation to lose your cool. If the other TV 'victim' loses his or her temper, that is that person's problem. You should stay calm, using your key messages to frame your argument logically.

Don't let the interviewer or an opponent interrupt you before you've managed to finish your answer; if needs be, pull the person up by pausing slightly and saying something like: 'If I might be allowed to continue and answer your question.' On the other hand, when your opponent is making a point that you disagree with, you can use the studio medium to express your disagreement. Don't say anything, just start shaking your head slowly, with a sad smile, as though to say: 'I'm afraid you're mistaken there.' You will effectively state, using body language, that you feel more sorrow than anger at this point, and you will cause one of two reactions: you will either give the producer in the gallery an opportunity to cut from the speaker to you shaking your head; alternatively, your opponent may get so rattled and interrupt the flow of his or her speech to say something like: 'And it's no good Fred Bloggs sitting there shaking his head, he knows I'm right.' In the latter case, you will have won the point. The little light on your camera will go on and you can use the opportunity to push in an extra key message to knock your opponent's argument down.

At the end of the interview, whether it's a one-to-one or debate format, the interviewer will act as the chair and probably do a brief summing up. You will have been told that the last question was coming up, via either a verbal cue ('And, finally, perhaps you could tell us . . .') or a signal from the floor manager (not dissimilar to somebody cutting across the throat or drawing circles in the air with the tip of one finger). If, during that summing up, you feel *strongly* that you are being unfairly maligned, you will have to act quickly. While your mike is still live, say something succinct, like 'You're still wrong' or even 'Nonsense!'. It's not perfect but you will stop your opponent having the last (negative) word on the subject. So:

Interviewer: So, there we must leave it, but it's fairly clear that, despite all that Mr Bloggs says, his garage is going to destroy the Newtown countryside once and for all.

You: Rubbish!

Interviewer: Back to you, Michael.

Only use this technique when you feel you are being wronged. It is very effective because the producer won't have time to open up the debate again, as the next item/interview will be cued up and ready to go. At the same time, you can ensure that the audience sees that your interviewer is trying to get away with being judge and jury.

Debates aside, you will probably find that using the SMOK method is as effective for dealing with TV interviews as it is for radio interviews. If you can, stay on the floor or by a monitor when you have finished, and watch the rest of the show. How do other people cope with the interview? What techniques or key points do they use? Is there anything you could steal for next time?!

When the final credits are rolling, *then* you can have a drink – you deserve it!

CHAPTER 7
Tried and Tested Stories

How to use them

If I was trying to sell this chapter in *Exchange & Mart*, my ad would probably read something like this:

> *For sale: press release story. Nearly 1000 previous owners but still very reliable. Used only every 12 months or so to avoid MOT (Monotony Or Tedium). Average space consumption: 10 column inches per edition.*

Well, perhaps that is a bit cynical. I wouldn't seriously compare your press releases with a second-hand Ford Escort. Nevertheless, there is a grain of truth here; most journalists will admit, after a few pints, that new stories – *genuinely* new – are few and far between. In practice, most 'news' stories and features tend to be old favourites – sort of journalistic retreads, to carry the motoring analogy further. Many of these golden oldies come around again and again. Yes, the details change – names, places and ages – but the headlines and the intro are virtually identical.

This applies as much to so-called 'hard' news coverage as to PR features such as those you offer in your press releases. How many times, for example, have you seen a picture story about an old-age pensioner (sorry, senior citizen) going for a swim in the Serpentine/English Channel on a freezing cold New Year's Day? Or 'having a go' with a walking stick when somebody foolishly tries to rob him or her? Or celebrating a Golden Wedding anniversary with the girl he met when they were both fourteen?

I could go on, and these are just the pensioner-type stories. Add a few more examples of different 'genres', such as 'human torch' horrors or vanishing vicars, and you can see how certain *types* of story crop up regularly. As one of the vicars may have said before he vanished: 'There is no new thing under the sun' (*Ecclesiastes* 1:8).

When I was a trainee reporter in London's East End, I remember well how excited I was when I was assigned to cover my first murder. But the details of the second one escape me now. And the third, fourth and fifth, frankly, all just blur into one. In other words, by the end of year two of my training, you could say that I had done 'murder stories' to death. I learnt that the techniques for writing a story are always the same, even for the ultimate 'hard news' story.

So, which 'tried and tested' stories are good, constructive publicity for your organisation? Have a quick look at those given in this chapter to see which story could inspire your first proper press release (see also the two stock stories given in Chapter 3). Be careful; each story must be used sparingly. *Once* a year is quite sufficient; otherwise your credibility starts to slip drastically with your 'customer', the journalists. MOT (Monotony Or Tedium) is *not* required, so don't be tempted to overdo it by using the same press release story twice in quick succession. And if you do, don't send it to the same journalist, thinking you'll get a second bite at the cherry.

Realistically, I would advise you to keep up a steady trickle of good but varied PR stories. Why not aim to get out at least one press release per month? As better ideas occur to you or those working in your organisation, you can perhaps think about moving up to two over, say, a typical four-week cycle. Anything more than that, however, is asking for trouble.

The last thing you want to do is to earn yourself a reputation as a time waster, and that is what could happen if you inundate your local paper with too much low-quality material. You are doing well if you send in only two good stories a month and see them both used. On the other hand, you are doing badly if you send in more than that and – surprise, surprise – nothing ever appears in print. You are wasting not only your time but everybody else's. News editors are not stupid people: they can spot a half-baked attempt at puff almost before it's out of the envelope.

Award story

We've already looked at one sort of award story in Chapter 5: the picture of you giving or receiving the 'big cheque'. Can you work up a different award story to suit your circumstances? If you are giving cash to a local youth club football team, why not get the cheque details written on a football? It's a novel picture, and the caption writers will have a 'ball' with gags about bouncing cheques.

An alternative idea is to set up your own award scheme as a means of winning coverage. If your company depends on a small number of key suppliers, for example, why not start a 'Supplier of the Year' award? This can take the shape of a cup or a shield, suitably engraved, which you can present to your favoured supplier. The cost of such a 'trophy' need not be expensive (check your local *Yellow Pages* for details of dealers) and the thing normally pays for itself in terms of the free editorial coverage that results.

You can either make the award ceremony a full-scale presentation, with staff on hand, perhaps, and refreshments for all, to create a bit of 'internal relations'; or you could literally just present it to the local media as a photocall, with you handing over the award at a set time to suit the local papers and your VIP supplier. Not only will this appeal to your local paper, it will also stand a good chance of winning a space in the local paper that serves your supplier's home town. If the supplier is also local, better still. Lay on your own photographer to cover the photocall so you have a picture to fall back on if the local paper fails to attend. The same picture can be sent to the trade press for increased coverage. Your press release should point out how Bloggs & Co have won the new Sharpsuit Corporation Supplier of the Year award against a field of XX other suppliers, and include a good quote from you explaining why quality suppliers are so important.

Whatever your business is, try to give a simple guide to the scale of your operation – something that the average person in the street can relate to. For example: 'Every year we use enough rubber hosing to run from here to Birmingham and back again.' Or: 'We manufacture so many soft drinks we could fill the Northtown Swimming Pool two hundred times a week.' A line or two to this effect will show what an impressive job your supplier has done to keep up with your output. It also saves churning out boring manufacturing statistics which, quite frankly, are only of interest to your production manager.

Schools, of course, tend to have at least one 'award story' a year – it's called a speech-day. Whether or not you have secured a 'personality' to present the prizes (see the next stock story for details), you should always invite the local newspaper. Speech-day is a showcase for the whole school – teachers, staff and pupils – so let the community know about it. If your event clashes with the press day for the local weekly paper, you are severely cutting the chances of the paper covering the event. It will probably be all hands on deck putting the week's paper 'to bed', and your event could fall foul of more contemporary material by the time the next edition is put together. So, take a chance and send the paper a copy of the main speech in advance, on the strict understanding that there is no coverage of the speech until a set time on a set date. For example, you could arrange it so that the speech, which is to be delivered at 7.30 on Thursday night, is delivered to the local paper the Monday before. By doing this, the paper can write a story based on the speech (as long as it's interesting enough) to appear in that Friday's paper. (In the next chapter, we look at how such arrangements, known as *embargoes*, can backfire. In the context of a school speech-day, however, there is little risk of this problem.)

A retailer with an eye to free publicity could use the 1000th customer (or some other milestone like 5000 or 10,000) as the basis for an award story. A trophy and a prize of some sort for the smiling punter will provide the ingredients of a good press release, especially with a black-and-white picture to match.

The personality

When in doubt, get somebody famous. Having a personality on hand can add appeal to a lot of your stories. Grand openings, not-so-grand reopenings and award stories like the examples given can all benefit from a well-known face. The question is, at what price?

You might be able to get certain local personalities free of charge for your event if you write a nice letter outlining your organisation's need and give plenty of advance notice (at least three months). Your local MP or the Mayor may respond favourably, for example, depending on the nature of your event and what exactly your organisation does. If you can get either of them, you have done well. Local papers normally get a copy of the Mayor's public engagements diary, so they effectively have two reasons to attend: your press release inviting them along, plus an 'official' reminder from the Town Hall.

Nationally recognised politicians could be another possibility. Again, plenty of notice will be required, and, if they accept your invitation, they will be prepared to join you free of charge, or for expenses only.

If you are more ambitious, you might try to get a TV or film star. Fine, but bear in mind that this idea may not turn out to be the cheap option. Be prepared to pay not only expenses but also a fee, depending on the stature or popularity of the personality. Charities can sometimes do a deal with a theatrical agent, which will mean a goodwill celebrity appearance free of charge; but for everybody else, it's a question of agreeing a budget and sticking to it.

If you can get a personality connected with your organisation in some way, so much the better. If you are a car dealer, for example, somebody like Murray Walker, the veteran motor racing commentator, would be a good choice. If you want a soap opera star (and they are very popular with the general public), you will need to establish who the agent is, the cost per hour and if the personality is available. Ring the station concerned during office hours (Granada for Coronation Street or the BBC at Elstree Studios for EastEnders, for example) and ask the production office for the agent's details. But be warned that such personal appearances by top soap opera stars can cost anything up to £1000. A cheaper alternative may be to go for a local celebrity – a sort of second-division star who happens to live near you (though don't put it quite that bluntly). The celebrity may or may not suggest that you talk to his or her agent to get things rolling, and, again, if it is a local event and yours is a good cause, the celebrity might be prepared to turn out for nothing.

Once you have got your personality, what will you do with him or her? Ribbon cutting is the old favourite, or pulling a cord to unveil a commemorative plaque. Alternatively, the personality could say a few words when presenting a prize or a cheque to a worthy cause on your behalf. If you choose this option, make sure that you provide the personality with an appropriate script and keep it simple as the personality probably won't have a chance to rehearse beforehand.

Otherwise, a good old-fashioned human interest picture is nice, with your celebrity surrounded by a few of your people and doing something visually interesting like cutting a cake or signing the visitors' book. The photographers will probably guide you on the best shot.

Animals and children

Don't for a second believe the old theatrical adage about never working with animals or children. When you are doing your own publicity, they are worth their weight in gold.

Animals first: dogs and cats are perhaps the most accessible for most of us, but don't rule out anything – from tropical spiders to pit ponies. All animals are highly photogenic, and you can provide plenty of caption material (laced with your key message) to accompany the shot.

Here are some examples to think about adapting:

- The insurance broker who introduced a discount for houses with resident dogs. The sales manager who originally thought of the idea was pictured outside his own home with his own dog.

- The disc jockey who took his dog into the studio because he found that his four-legged friend helped interviews to go better by putting guests at ease.
- The publican who thought his rural boozer was haunted, until he discovered that a cat had been sneaking in and playing on the pool-table at night.

Some people don't even use a real animal – a toy teddy bear can also make a nice picture, as in the case of a story about a charity parachutist who insisted on taking his teddy bear with him on the big day – and he wasn't too nervous to pose for the photographers before he went up! A similar story was about a women's guild who made teddy bears to raise cash for a local children's ward. An obliging nurse was pictured in the evening paper with a particularly cuddly example.

So, keep an eye and an ear out for any connection between your goods and services and members of the animal kingdom. You'll immediately have a good story on your hands. My favourite story is about some penguins in a Surrey zoo who were developing verrucas on their flippers. The keeper realised that the problem was due to some damp concrete surrounding the penguin pool and so he invested in some rubber mats to keep the area dry. Result: flippers free from verrucas, and as much publicity as the zoo and the rubber mat makers could handle!

Children are also very photogenic (given a little gentle persuasion and a discreet packet of sweets). Whether they are playing in your new company crèche, or dressed up in outlandish clothes left over from your record-breaking jumble sale, photographers love to capture the moment on film. Their editors know, of course, that every child that gets his or her picture in the paper will have several potential admirers: not just the parents, but grandparents and doting aunts and uncles, all of whom will probably buy at least one copy of the paper to keep for posterity.

So, from the newspaper's point of view, it makes sense to publish pictures of children to keep casual sales buoyant. Hamleys, the children's toyshop in London, is well aware of the appeal of picture stories involving children. When the Royal National Institute for the Blind organised a 'fun afternoon' for visually handicapped children to visit the store, the media were also allowed to join in the fun. The result was a lovely picture, on the front page of the *Guardian*, showing a seven-year-old girl playing with a kinetic plasma chamber (a visually interesting toy – a sort of orb with electrical waves moving inside it).

Sponsoring children to do something is another good local story. A Sussex-based weekly newspaper carried a piece about an engineering firm sponsoring a local 14-year-old boy who showed an aptitude for clay pigeon shooting. The company supplied the boy with clothing and cartridges for his sport and arranged a photocall to show him kitted out. A good-three-column picture resulted in the local weekly, with a glowing plug for the company thrown in. Everybody was happy – the paper, the boy and the sponsors who spotted his talent. For minimal expense, the engineering firm thus achieved good local coverage.

World's first?

The world's first anything is worth the attention of a few journalists, as is the first 'whatever' in Britain. As such things are difficult to prove sometimes, the convention is to produce a press release saying something like:

> The new software package, thought to be the first in Britain produced exclusively for use by undertakers, will speed up administration at Newtown-based funeral directors Gildersons.

Likewise, any specialised equipment that you purchase overseas which is very unusual in the UK could merit a trade press release. And if you have anything that you feel merits a place in the *Guinness Book of Records*, don't keep it to yourself. When you write to Guinness Publishing Ltd with your submission (address in *The Writer's Handbook*), do a press release as well. *The Guinness Book of Records* is the world's highest-selling copyright book. So, if your organisation is being considered for an entry, make sure that you get your share of decent exposure out of the fact!

Charity booster

Anything you do to assist a charity, either corporately or individually, is worth a press release. It could be that a member of your staff is doing something outlandish, such as having a sponsored bath to raise cash for a good cause. Or you could be giving a product/service free of charge to help with a specific need. Invariably, the charity will be willing to co-operate; apart from anything else, it will appreciate the value of free publicity as a means of generating other donations.

The launch

The launch is associated mainly with new products, and is a tried and tested basis for a press release. Just as a company launches a new product or service, a school can launch a new initiative to attract more pupils, or a charity can launch a new drive for sponsorship. In each case, the intro should include the expression 'launch a new' something. In practice, of course, the launch could be no more than a press release and some new literature which can be photographed. The important thing is that whatever you are launching must be *genuinely* new and not just something you already offer. Providing a picture of the new product, or somebody using the new service, is always good practice.

The Department of Trade and Industry (DTI) operates a 'New Products from Britain' (NPFB) service which helps British companies to test and promote products overseas, by encouraging editors of magazines and journals to carry editorial features. The DTI points out that the service is not a paid-for publicity service, like advertising, but that its aim is to achieve editorial coverage about the products in the appropriate publications in those countries that you are trying to reach.

The NPFB service offers experienced journalists from the Central Office of Information (COI) to write the story, using press release and other publicity material which you supply. You check the text for factual accuracy, and it is then translated, if appropriate, into the language of the countries that you are aiming at, through the Diplomatic Service posts. The 'posts' aim to place the story in suitable publications, and you will be sent a list of the media targeted. The DTI charges for this service, which is one of a range of services to encourage and assist UK exporters. Your local DTI office can provide details; the number will be in the phone book.

Another very useful vehicle for launching publicity for new products is the BBC World Service. Funded by the government, the BBC World Service was, in 1989, the fifth largest international broadcasting service in the world, in number of hours of programming per week. The BBC claims that the service has the largest number of regular listeners.

The regular programmes of most interest to you are, first, *New Ideas*, a radio shop-window for new products and inventions, which goes out four times a week. Second, there is *Business Matters*, a weekly survey of commercial and financial news (good for new products, but also for 'order' stories, outlined next). The others to bear in mind are: *From the Weeklies*, which goes out three times on Saturdays, providing a review of the British weekly press (where, of course, your stories will be appearing regularly!) and *Science in Action*, which is a review of progress in science, technology and medicine.

The 'launch' story is closely related to the 'breakthrough' story, which is of most use to manufacturing companies. The intro goes something like this: 'A design breakthrough has meant that the Well Heeled Shoe Company has now produced a pair of trainers that float on water.' The actual mechanics of the breakthrough are kept to a bare minimum, well down the page. There are two reasons for this: you don't want to bore the reader with technical details, and you don't want your rivals to glean so much of your technology that it is easy for them to copy you!

The order

With any luck, within a few months of your press release about the new product launch, you will have more good news – details of the first major order. This may be at home or overseas. Whatever the case, it will show that your company is successfully 'doing the business'. If it is a major order, the question the media are sure to ask you is: 'How many jobs will it create?' Have your answer ready; if you will cope with the order by just taking on a few casual helpers over the summer holidays, then say so – don't give the impression that permanent jobs will follow if this is not the case.

The other pitfall is premature talk. Wait until the contract is signed, sealed and delivered before anybody in your organisation starts talking about it; there are few things more embarrassing than something impressive falling through at the last minute. The best you can hope for is no coverage at all – potentially, you could get a bad press. Remember, reporters are on the look-out for any news story they can get. They are just as happy to run a bad news piece along the lines of 'Newtown Engineering fails to win important French contract' as your alternative good news story. So, keep the deal close to your corporate chest until all is well, and then let the world know about it!

Topical

This is the one you can't see coming until it arrives. It could be that, unlike the other set pieces, you never get the chance to take advantage of a topical story. Essentially, it is the result of news and current events (way beyond your control) which happen to affect your organisation directly.

I once came across a small company selling filter hoods for passengers on airlines to prevent smoke inhalation in the event of a fire. The hoods not only enabled the passengers to breathe without inhaling too many fumes, but they also had a Perspex front so people could see their way to safety. The company had already done a product launch press release and picture, and had had some success. But then, some months later, there was a major air disaster involving a plane catching fire. The company owners immediately saw the topical value of their product. They were quoted as saying that many airlines are now considering the introduction of fire filter hoods and that some casualties may have been avoided had products such as theirs been on board.

The company won both local and national publicity by acting quickly and providing a new 'angle' on the air disaster story.

Obviously, there was no way that anybody could have foreseen the air disaster. And there was a good chance that the hood suppliers may never have been able to promote their product in this way. But, as it happens, an event at the other side of the world enabled them to create an opportunity for favourable, free publicity.

Regional media outlets are always looking for their angle on the stories in the nationals, so if you can provide one, they will be genuinely grateful. If you or a member of your team has any connection with a major news story, consider letting your local newspaper know about it. The same goes for any product relevance. The important thing is that you act quickly.

A press release in this situation is probably not the best method of spreading your message. It may take you too long to draft it and clear it internally. It's better to just ring the local media outlets (when you are quite sure of your angle to the story) and let them interview you.

It need not be a disaster to make a topical story happen for your organisation; it could be that you have supplied something that is being used by somebody famous who is in the news for some reason. David Bowie's song, 'Space Oddity', sums this up neatly. It's about an astronaut drifting in space who is told by radio that 'the papers want to know whose shirts you wear'. If the shirt company had already got its publicity act together, the papers wouldn't need to ask – they would already know! (This kind of story will often spring naturally from a sponsorship package.)

Nostalgia/anniversary

Newspapers are funny things. On the same page, you will quite often see a story about something which has just taken place, and slap bang next to it is a feature about something that happened '50 years ago today'.

Anniversary stories are the way you can cash in on the need for the occasional nostalgic piece. If your organisation has been around for some years, you can generate coverage fairly easily if you have a bench-mark anniversary coming up. 'This week sees the thirtieth anniversary of Northtown's first comprehensive school' could be the intro you are looking for. Time is on your side with these stories, so why not approach the news editor at your local paper to sound out the ideas?

Many local papers like running pictures of 'yester-year', so you could give them an excuse to raid their files – and yours – for some interesting old stuff.

Some companies are actually in the business of nostalgia and so they have a head start. I once came across a firm that specialised in restoring old Morris Minors and selling them. The owner realised the affection that the public had for his 'product' and used it continually for winning coverage. Every year or so seemed to be an anniversary of some sort: either 50 years since the prototype Morris was introduced or 25 years since the last Morris rolled off the production line.

Sensibly, the company also used new developments to win decent exposure. It once introduced a 'wolf in sheep's clothing' to the market: what looked like the average Morris Minor but with a powerful engine and up-graded suspension. This version was at home in the fast lane on the motorway, and the company took full advantage of the 'breakthrough' (see earlier) for publicity purposes. Almost every motoring magazine, plus a generous cross-section of national newspaper motoring writers, ran a piece. It even made the network news on TV.

Everybody can make the nostalgia story work for them. If you are in retailing, can you use the fiftieth birthday of your shop to sell something at the price you sold it at 50 years ago? If you are celebrating an anniversary at a school, can some of the pupils dress up in a period school uniform for a photocall?

Long service

Again, this is a nice human interest story, ideal for a picture treatment. If somebody in your organisation has been with you for a significant period of time, then why not institute a long-service award of your own? A trophy or memento could be presented by you or your management representative, and you could have your photographer on hand to capture the moment. Your picture caption should include details like: the length of service, what the job involves and how old the person was when he or she joined. A period of, say, 25 years with the same organisation deserves some recognition; it reflects well on both the employee and the employer.

CHAPTER 8
More Follows . . .

Introduction

Dealing with journalists effectively is clearly a key part of your free publicity operation. You've seen how they need you as a contact just as much as you need them. But there are still certain ground rules that you have to take on board – you ignore them at your peril!

In this chapter, we look at the conventions which have grown up to protect both you and the journalist from misunderstandings. Yes, I know, there are some journalists who are out-and-out 'stitch-up' merchants, but they really are few and far between. And, frankly, they're not worth dwelling on; no ground rules will stop them from writing an inaccurate piece, which could be a disappointment to you. However, in my experience, such short-term hacks can't operate for long. More often than not, an embarrassing or unfavourable piece is caused by a simple breakdown in communication, which is a two-way process. As ever, the onus is on you (the interviewees) to make sure that they (the interviewers) get it right. So, you might like to think of these conventions as a safety net to help you to avoid the most common problems before they occur.

Also covered in this chapter are two detailed case studies from weekly publications. The first is from a successful national women's magazine, *Bella*, and the second appeared in a well-respected, local, paid-for newspaper, the *Reading Chronicle*. In their own field, each of them is a fairly typical publication. The two companies featured in the articles were happy to pass on their advice, so it's worth comparing your ideas with theirs.

Lastly, we will look at how your organisation might be able to provide editors with something else they need – that is, apart from good news and feature material. Reader competitions build circulation for paid-for titles, and help 'bonding' (or reader affiliation) for the freesheets. From your point of view, a successful promotion of this kind can effectively combine the benefits of PR and advertising, and at minimal cost to you.

Playing by the rules

Off-the-record

We saw in Chapter 6 how it is best to treat every microphone as live, just in case you make a joke or an off-hand remark that is recorded and used out of context. The same 'safety first' motto applies when you are talking to journalists, casually, face to face perhaps, or on the phone. Unless otherwise agreed, any interview with a reporter should be treated as on-the-record; in other words, you can be quoted directly on anything you say. If for some reason you decide that you wish to give your journalist some sensitive background material, say, or to illustrate a point that you don't want quoted, then you (or the reporter) can opt to go *off-the-record*. This means that anything you say is for information only, not for use. A reporter will often try to entice you to go off-the-record when he or she can see you are being cagey about something. Alternatively, *you* may decide it is easier to talk off-the-record. Either way, you *must both agree* before you start talking freely, or serious misunderstandings could follow.

More than once I have come across an instance of a reporter who has discovered the best story going, but only by going off-the-record. This means that the reporter can't use it, except perhaps to store it away for future use. Grumble and groan as they may, they have all honoured the convention nevertheless.

Problems tend to occur when an interview has started as *on*-the-record, but changes to *off*-the-record. Then, a bit further into the interview still, something is said that would make a good story, but it is still covered by the off-the-record agreement. Even if it interrupts your flow a little, you must state the basis on which you are talking. Once again, have your own tape recorder handy to ensure that you have a record of what was said and on what basis. Nine out of ten journalists will respect this convention, but you could find yourself talking to the tenth one who doesn't, so it's a good idea to have your own version of what was said.

Non-attribution

Non-attribution is another useful device. While off-the-record means that the material cannot be used at all, non-attributable material *can* be used, but it must not be attributed to you. The details you pass on are written in such a way as to avoid revealing the source of the information. Once such an undertaking is given, most journalists will go to extreme lengths to honour it. A short while ago, a trainee reporter on a technical magazine, *The Engineer*, found himself in contempt of court for refusing to reveal the source of one of his stories. In the end, he was fined, but he stood in the dock willing to risk prison in order not to break his word.

Embargo

Less dramatic, but equally important in its own way, is the embargo. A press release issued under embargo means that you are passing on details of a story on the condition that they are not used before a certain date or time. This can help you operationally (as in the school speech-day example, Chapter 7). Again, it relies on a degree of trust. National newspapers have been known to break embargoes for reasons that can only be described as mischievous; local newspapers have been known to do the same thing through sloppiness, pure and simple. It is best to avoid using embargoes if you possibly can. If you have no choice, write in capital letters at the top of your press release:

ISSUED UNDER STRICT EMBARGO: DO NOT USE BEFORE (add date)

and put at the bottom of the release (where your further contact details are):

PLEASE NOTE EMBARGO . . . PLEASE NOTE EMBARGO . . .

By doing this, nobody reading the press release can say they didn't realise!

Exclusive

There is one last 'trust game' which you should be aware of – the exclusive. Although the term has become somewhat debased, especially by the tabloids, an exclusive basis still gives your story additional cachet. If you honour it (and the other newspapers don't just nick it once the first editions are out), the newspaper you are dealing with will effectively have the story all to itself. Unlike the embargo and working off-the-record, it is *your* honesty that is at stake here, not the journalist's. Make the decision to offer the story exclusively to one of your better contacts and then stick to your guns. Don't start touting it around what used to be known as Fleet Street.

The advantage of the exclusive is that you stand a very good chance of doing 'a deal' and seeing your story in print. The disadvantage is that you are automatically reducing your chance of getting the story used elsewhere; others might have given it an even better treatment in terms of space (or maybe not – but you'll never know!).

When a freelance journalist contributes a story on an exclusive basis, he or she gets paid more for it. So, if your contribution will help you to cement a good relationship with a particular news room contact, then the exclusive is well worth considering. Don't, however, leave your contact thinking that you will always be so obliging. And look for something in return, later (perhaps a mention for your next press release). Such give-and-take is the stuff of many successful relationships between the publicist and the reporter.

Case study 1

Organisation: Charity Recruitment

Business: Staff recruitment for charities

Periodical:	*Bella* (women's magazine, circulation 1.3 million)
Nature of piece:	Feature in the 'Women at Work' series; about 500 words long, bylined, and with a small black-and-white picture. The piece included a contact telephone number, which was unfortunately misprinted.
Method:	Charity recruitment co-founder Olga Johnson placed the feature by sending in a press release, which was also used in the *Daily Telegraph* and the *Financial Times*.
Approach:	The article emphasised how there was a new agency catering expressly for the needs of workers seeking to join charities. Charity Recruitment recognises that Britain's 162,000 charities are also a business, and that recruiting the right people is an important job.

'*Bella* rang us up shortly after we issued the press release', explained Olga Johnson. 'We gave a breakdown of the sort of salaries that charities paid, pointing out how they were on average about 20 per cent less than the going rate.'

The picture – Olga with one of her major clients – was sent in with the press release. It wasn't used 'big', perhaps because the story was a difficult one to illustrate effectively. But the words themselves were good.

Olga believes in the power of the follow-up. She said: 'Whenever we manage to get editorial support, we always drop the writer a line afterwards, telling them how grateful we are and promising to keep them informed of developments.'

She is also a great believer in using quality stationery, not just for press releases but also for general correspondence. 'The impression you create is very important', she said. 'When I started Charity Recruitment, I was working out of a spare bedroom at home. But because I used quality stationery, people were left with the impression that we were a bigger organisation than we really were. I actually got a letter asking if there was a job going at our headquarters office!'

The content of Olga's press release was a variation on the survey story. Using her own data, Olga worked out what sort of salary somebody working for a charity would get compared to a similar job in commerce. The press release also gave figures on the number of charities in the UK, showing the range of jobs available, and explained briefly how it was more cost effective for charities to use her agency than advertise for staff themselves. (I got the impression that this was a secondary message however; first and foremost was the theme that women could contact the agency to find a satisfying career structure.)

Olga also makes a point of talking to editors of charity magazines as they are appointed, to help cultivate goodwill. 'I then find that they are genuinely pleased if we are prepared to write an article for them – it's a question of approaching them in the right way.'

Olga's piece in *Bella* gave details (at the end) for readers to follow up, which is a useful response mechanism. Despite the fact that the phone number was missing a digit, the address details were good enough for anyone to check with directory enquiries and establish contact. Getting your phone number in is very much a bonus, as more often than not sub-editors will take it out: (a) because of a lack of space and (b) because they feel that a phone number makes *their* story look a bit too much like *your* advertisement. *Bella*, though, clearly realised that some readers would be interested in moving to a charity and were thus prepared to include the contact details as a service to them.

Case study 2

Organisation:	Hop Inn
Business:	Small, Berkshire-based off-licence
Periodical:	*Reading Chronicle* (average circulation 30,000)
Nature of piece:	Large picture story showing the exterior of the off-licence, with seven paragraphs of text.

Method: Owner Brian McEntee was contacted by the advertising section at the *Reading Chronicle*, who spoke to the news room on his behalf.

Approach: Brian found that the *Reading Chronicle* was supportive of his off-licence business, with the advertising section offering to act as a go-between with the editorial side.

This particular story was about a new branch of the off-licence which Brian and his wife Gie were opening. To promote the store, they gave away free beer to the new customers.

Brian said: 'I've found that the advertising section of the local paper has a good relationship with the editorial side, which can help enormously. For that reason, I have never needed to contact the editorial people direct, although they always make it clear that advertising doesn't mean automatic free coverage.'

Brian has advertised widely in the past but now keeps it to a minimum. 'I found it hard to establish what I was getting for the money', he said. 'I also noticed that if I got an editorial write-up in one of the local papers, the customers would mention it to me – but they wouldn't mention if they had seen an ad or not.'

With this in mind, Brian set about winning some good, free coverage in the shape of an April Fool's joke: 'One year we decided we would have a laugh with some of the local customers', he explained. 'On April first, we blacked out the windows of the shop and put up signs saying: "Opening Soon: Sex Shop". I made sure I wrote to both the local papers and I even dropped a line to some of the national press. That story really put the shop on the map. We got the front page of one local paper, the back page of the other, and a mention in one of the national tabloids. By the time some of the locals had worked up a petition of protest, they were reading how they had been had!'

Brian has also managed to generate an interview on the local BBC TV station, using the fact that he supplied bulk orders for a local beer festival. He also persuaded the local independent radio station, Radio 210, to send a disc jockey to cover the opening of his first shop.

'The story about the sex shop joke was picked up by one of the trade papers as well, though frankly I find that of limited use. I don't really want others stealing my good ideas!' he said.

He also said: 'The other reason I don't go overboard on advertising is the fact I have extremely localised customers; I don't really need to speak to the entire population of Reading, when I am really only aiming at people living in the vicinity of the shops. For that reason, I prefer to use free publicity and leaflets to get the promotions over.'

Competitions

Successful competitions are worth their weight in gold, as Brian found out during the run-up to the Royal Wedding of Charles and Diana. 'It was as though everybody was going Royalty mad and all the papers were full of it', said Brian. 'We were selling a special bottled ale with a commemorative label, and I contacted the editor of the weekly paper with a suggestion. I provided about 50 bottles of the Royal label ales for a reader's competition, which the paper ran. That was useful publicity, and the response was excellent – hundreds of people wrote in to take part. When the editor had selected the winner, the paper arranged for a photographer to cover me handing the prizes over. It cost us very little, but generated an awful lot of goodwill', he said.

The Royal Wedding helped in this case but a competition is worth considering at any time. The first stage is to write to the editor of your chosen publication with your suggestions. You will need to offer an attractive prize (or prizes) to generate reader response, and, obviously, it should be relevant to your organisation if at all possible. If you suggest a format that is acceptable, the editor will generally give the feature a reasonable space, with a picture of your prize, plus a brief write-up about it and a mention of the fact that you have donated it. Such promotions are so popular with weekly papers that they often get an additional plug on the front page as part of the 'flash' showing the week's attractions.

The format of the competition itself can vary. I have found that a word-grid is popular, as it is not too difficult to complete, and it appeals to the many readers who like crossword-type puzzles. Typically, a word-grid is made up of 144 letters chosen apparently at random. Hidden within the grid are certain words, which can be detected written forwards or backwards, up or down, vertically, horizontally or diagonally. The reader draws a line around the keywords, cuts out the form and sends it into the paper or magazine.

You will need to give a cut-off date for entries and state that the first three correct answers out of the hat will receive a prize each. Obviously, the more prizes that can be won, the heavier the response you will get. The competition may be run over two weeks (if the prize is really attractive), but more often you will find that your goods or services enjoy a nice spread for very little outlay.

With all such competitions, the editor's decision is final, so you should let the editor choose the winner. You might offer, however, to take all the entry forms off his hands afterwards; they could be of use to you as a potential mailing list for future, direct mail-type promotions, and the newspaper won't want to keep them.

Don't forget to arrange for the picture desk to be tipped off when the lucky winners receive the prizes. You can then get more coverage in the following week's paper. And remember to keep the competition simple. If it is too complex, people won't enter and the editor will be disappointed with the low response.

Possibly one of the best competitions I have come across was linked to an interesting story in the *Sun*. A chocolate manufacturer claimed to have found a way of making its product a powerful aphrodisiac by adding extra cocoa. Not only did the paper give full details, it also added its own 'give-away' – ten baskets of the special chocolates to the readers who wrote in with the best romantic stories.

Another favourite of mine was a story about a repro furniture company who allowed its 'antique' desks to be featured in a 'guess the value' competition run by the *Sunday Express*. This in itself was worth a picture caption in the local newspaper. So, without actually giving anything away, the company got both national and local publicity for a competition that didn't cost a bean!

Bear this in mind if you succeed in selling a competition idea to a national publication; your friendly local newspaper reporter would like to hear about it. In the free publicity game, nothing succeeds like success!

CHAPTER 9
And Now . . . the Bad News

Negative coverage/bad publicity

All publicity is good publicity – right? Well, up to a point. I would prefer to say *most* publicity is good publicity, because free media exposure is a two-edged sword.

This book sets out primarily to spread the 'good news': how your organisation can win valuable, constructive coverage to improve your corporate image through sustained, successful PR. Having said that, it's as well to make you aware of the risks as well as the opportunities that follow.

PR is not just about circulating your successful cuttings and enjoying expense account lunches with pet 'journos'. There is a down side, and in this chapter we think about the unthinkable – negative coverage and bad publicity.

Imagine this: your organisation – whatever it may be – suddenly finds itself in deep trouble. Not only that, but, to cap it all, the press are already on to it.

I'm sure you don't need me to outline the range of possible corporate nightmares, but here are some examples:

- Financial: cash goes missing together with one of your directors or partners/poor results combined with rumours/ speculation about your future.
- Personnel problems: you may have to close a factory or shop/ suffer redundancies/face an industrial tribunal.
- Personal problems: a member of your staff is involved in sex/ drugs scandal and/or police enquiries.
- Emergency/accident: an explosion in the works with injuries

or fatalities/a major road traffic accident involving one of your company's vans.

- Product: a health scare over one of your products/sabotage by a pressure group/a disgruntled and vocal customer threatens to take you to the cleaners.

All the above are 'news' – the sort that interests journalists and sells newspapers.

The fact that each of these is also a major headache for you and bad news for your organisation is neither here nor there. Each of the scenarios listed may lead to unsolicited media attention, possibly on a scale which makes all your constructive PR achievements look a bit paltry.

It's a salutary thought, but the same local newspaper that spared you a miserable two paragraphs when you pulled off a major overseas contract will probably give any one of these stories the 'big' treatment, perhaps the front page.

And that's just the local damage. It can get worse. Many local reporters, if they have any journalistic nous at all, will recognise a major story and realise two things:

1. It deserves a wider readership.
2. They can make money (and possibly enhance their career prospects) by 'selling' it to their colleagues on the national newspapers. This practice, although officially discouraged by newspaper editors, goes on nevertheless.

We look at the logistics of this later, but the main point here is that a bad press at any level is still a bad press. Trying to dismiss the fact with a shrug and the thought 'Oh well, it's only the local rag' is a serious mistake. In the PR arena complacency is akin to recklessness.

So, given that the harsh glare of negative publicity will at some point head your way, the question is: What do you do about it?

The ostrich school of thought

The ostrich school of thought tackles this problem by pretending that nothing is wrong. Comforting, yes, but only in the short term. Here is a scenario which explores the possible consequences of such myopia.

Your local paper has somehow found out about, say, the health scare over one of your products. The reporter who tries to reach you is a stranger to you. He's certainly not the nice chap you have been 'cultivating' as an outlet for your (favourable) stories in the weekly paper. So, because you fear the worst, the reporter's initial phone call is never returned; furthermore, secretaries are instructed to say that you are in a meeting and cannot be disturbed, whenever they get calls from the press.

Any good work you've done with your local press contacts will immediately start to suffer if you suddenly clam up. And, with a major bad news story such as this one, the chances are that you will no longer be dealing with your friendly local media contacts.

Suddenly, you (or whoever you have asked to help stall the press) get phone calls from other media outlets asking for a 'comment' – the regional evening paper and the local radio station – and they are not so polite about asking. If they too are given the white lie about you being tied up in a very important meeting, you could be heading for serious problems, Mr Ostrich.

A group of reporters from the national press, perhaps the tabloids, may not be fobbed off quite so easily. Instead, they could attempt to 'doorstep' you, the journalist's equivalent of the salesperson's 'foot in the door', only without the charm. In practice, it means they will camp outside your office, or even your home, until you submit to their intimidating demands for an interview.

In no time at all, cameras are everywhere. Mrs Ostrich daren't step outside the door to pick up the milk for fear of running the media gauntlet. A group of photographers are standing by to take whatever picture they can of you and your family. A reporter friend of mine once described them as the 'Nikon choir', inspired no doubt by the sound of a dozen 'autowinds' whirring in unison. And that's just the photographers.

The rest of the media have obtained your home phone number from somewhere (probably the local telephone book, or directory enquiries) and they ring continually with their questions. A stream of notes is constantly pushed through the door, demand-ing an interview. Phrases like 'in the public interest' are used.

If you know something that the media wish to report on, they will do *anything* in their power to get you to talk. They will beg, cajole, threaten, plead, as long as whichever method they use gives them access to you before their deadline, and, ideally, after everybody else's. (Incidentally, the journalists' trade paper, *UK Press Gazette*, has a weekly column called 'Dog Watches Dog' that is always full of gloating 'scoop'-type tales.)

What the media would really like, and you must have seen examples of this yourself, is an act of 'unprovoked' aggression from you. Something like you waving a fist at the camera or, better still, swearing at them as you reach the end of your tether. This makes good copy and, most damning of all, a nice picture. It confirms your guilt immediately in public perception terms when they add the incident to their report, along the lines that:

> *We tried to put these questions to Mr Ostrich, who immediately went into hiding. When the* Daily Orbit *tracked down Ostrich to his luxury £200,000 Surrey home, he swore at us and threatened to assault* Orbit *cameraman Sid Righteous.*

What they won't mention is that the *Daily Orbit* was just one representative of a pack of journalists pursuing you for all you were worth, and making your life a misery. Not only will you and your family have had an extremely unpleasant experience, but you will have failed to put across your side of the story (whatever it may be) and so have been found guilty, by default.

In other words, never mind the facts, the details or the mitigating circumstances, you're simply too late. The PR damage to your organisation has already been done.

Such sharp tactics have been used again and again by news-hungry journalists, who, after all, are only trying to do their job to the best of their ability. They want to provide information, and they want to provide it quickly because, quite simply, that's what news is.

By the way, don't rely on the police to keep the press pack at bay for you. You'll quickly discover that these journalists are not committing an offence by merely attempting to interview you.

And if they wish to camp out near your home with their zoom lenses trailed on your front door, well, it's a free country. Even the laws of trespass won't help you in this scenario; trespass is a civil matter, not a criminal one, and certainly not one for the local constabulary.

To put it bluntly, your home may be your castle, but if you fail to handle the press properly, you may well end up under siege.

For a first-hand experience of being on the receiving end of this sort of treatment by the press, read *Stalker*. Disregarding the subject matter, Mr Stalker's recollection of an unremitting media 'barrage' is by no means untypical. Even those of us who are not normally in the public eye could expect similar treatment if we suddenly find ourselves thrust into the spotlight. And don't expect to be wooed by reporters bearing cheque books; they are normally for the already rich and famous/infamous.

So, how do you handle the hacks from Hades in this situation? Well, you've probably guessed the answer already: *avoid the situation in the first place*. First, let's play the role-reversal game and consider the scenario from the journalist's point of view.

The journalist's point of view

The chain of thought now goes like this: a person who can provide a news story for your readers (or viewers and listeners) is refusing to co-operate. Why? What has he got to hide?

You are planning a short but balanced piece, with background, to explain the issues to your readers, who you know will be interested; if anything, this man has been wronged and this fact may provide the 'angle' for the story. Leaving aside the question of accuracy, surely this man will co-operate if only to clear his own name? It's your job – nay, your duty as a conscientious journalist – to give him every opportunity to put his side of the story. And, if he suddenly becomes abusive, well, that's a story in itself, isn't it – especially if there is no other material to work with?

In short, journalists want you to help them with their news story. But if you won't co-operate, there is no way they will just turn around the film crew and go back to their news editors empty-handed. The fact is, they are often going to do the story anyway, with or without your co-operation.

Crisis management

Imagine that you are a small local dairy, and, for the sake of the argument, a carton of your milk has been discovered with bleach in it.

Such an incident will be reported to various 'authorities' (the police if sabotage is suspected, the local public health officer, the Ministry of Agriculture, Fisheries and Food; all these spring to mind, although there are probably others). The person who actually made the discovery (drank the milk) may have done so too late, in which case the local hospital will also be aware of what has happened.

Some, or all, of these authorities will be prepared to talk about the incident to the press. They have nothing to lose, and probably feel a genuine need to provide information for the public via the news media. Apart from anything else, they will look to publicity to ensure that the incident won't be repeated.

The news media could, therefore, be in possession of a number of facts, which they see as the basis of a perfectly reasonable story, before they even try to contact you. What they don't know, they may well speculate about as a means of adding to their copy. And what they speculate about could be even worse than the actual facts.

These questions (and others) will need some sort of answer: Do you use bleach to clean your milking equipment? Is this incident the result of your neglect? How many pints of milk could be poisoned? What are you doing to stop people buying the suspect pints? Will you throw away all of tomorrow's milk as a result? Are you the subject of a blackmail threat?

If you don't provide the real facts, there's a risk that nobody will. All right, so *you* know you're innocent, but nobody else does. The onus is on you to tell the media the facts, and as quickly as possible. One reporter's mistakes and/or speculation can be picked up by another and echoed as fact, especially in the heat of the moment, and if you are hiding your head in the sand.

Suppose you have had a phone call from a group claiming responsibility for the bleach, so vindicating your tank-cleaning operation as the reason for the incident. By making yourself available and telling the media this, you are making the best of a bad situation. At least you will arrest some of the wilder misinformation, and, as a bonus of sorts, you may even be able to create some corporate sympathy.

I'm not saying this is easy; you would need to pluck up your courage. And you're right, a radio reporter who wants to grill you on air about the bleach you have allegedly put in your milk by mistake can make your palms sweat. But if you give the reporter something that will make a better story, there is no reason at all why he or she shouldn't give your dairy a reasonable and sympathetic treatment as a by-product of your co-operation. But the reporter certainly won't be able to do that if you're hiding in the garden shed.

This area, known as *crisis management*, has emerged as a major element of corporate strategy in larger companies. For smaller organisations and businesses, however, the discipline of thinking the unthinkable and planning accordingly is either unheard of or totally disregarded.

Of course, in a crisis, we would all rather get on with sorting it out than telling the press what a predicament we are in. But think of the ramifications if you avoid media enquiries. The facts may be distressing, but speculation could be even worse, and is sure to cause more problems.

So, what should a small organisation do to manage its as yet unknown crisis properly, at least in PR terms? This is a difficult situation to tackle as you don't know when a crisis is going to strike, or what the crisis will be. The answer lies in *PR contingency plans*, which can be called into play as soon as you realise you are facing a critical situation.

PR contingency plans

Your PR contingency plans should be as versatile as possible, because you will have other things to deal with if and when the crisis strikes.

Use the following guidelines to help you to prepare for trouble. With any luck, you'll never need them!

1. Nominate a spokesperson.

This should be somebody who knows your operation well and ideally has at some stage in the past performed radio/TV interviews (see Chapter 6). This person will be the first point of contact for the media, and so should be informed of developments as they occur. By nominating a spokesperson for the organisation, you will free other members of your team to handle the issue itself; all 'stray' media enquiries should be politely but firmly pointed towards the spokesperson.

2. Prepare an organisation profile/fact sheet.

This should be a single sheet of A4, typed press release style (see Chapter 3), complete with your company/organisation logo as the mast-head. The heading should be something like 'Background Sheet'. It should answer, at a glance, questions such as these:

- When was the company/organisation established?
- Where is it based?
- What does it do? (It's a good discipline to express this in one concise and accurate paragraph; use your key message.)
- How many people are employed by your organisation?
- Brief details of any community involvement/charity work/ sponsorship.
- Brief details of any corporate successes (major deals/ achievements).
- Previous year's financial results (if applicable).
- Telephone number/fax number for nominated spokesperson.

At the first whiff of trouble, this company profile press release should be sent to journalists hungry for facts about your organisation. You cannot assume that the journalists who already know your background will be the same journalists chasing the current story.

3. Brief the Press Association.

Your nominated spokesperson should make it his or her first job to issue the company profile to the Press Association, prefixed with a short statement summing up the current state of play.

The Press Association (PA) is effectively a wholesaler of news. It is paid for by a consortium of local newspapers around the country who require a comprehensive news service. The national stories carried by your local evening paper are more often than not provided by the PA. And it is a PA correspondent who should be offered your information first. Often, the PA has regional correspondents. Find out who yours is and keep his or her number to hand.

The PA correspondent will turn your information into news 'copy' and effectively syndicate it widely, thus providing all the other journalists with the 'core information' they need to cover the story. And, from a corporate point of view, this is perhaps the smartest move of all. PA correspondents work to the highest standards of journalism, providing accurate and balanced copy to punishing deadlines.

If PA copy is pouring into the news rooms of the country via the 'tapes' (or, these days, thrown directly on to monitors), telling the (correct) current company story, then the chances are that most news organisations won't need any other information – at least in the short term. True, you will get some newspapers following up the PA copy and wanting to talk to you direct. But the chances are that they will start to chase the story from other sources instead, if 'PA has already spoken to the company'. Also, don't forget that broadcast news journalists (radio and TV) will still want an interview, although they may be able to use some of your information for hourly bulletins in the meantime.

Some outlets (perhaps the local weekly papers and the trade press) do not take PA copy. For these outlets, your nominated spokesperson could send the company profile details by fax, and then take other enquiries when the journalists concerned have briefed themselves. The strength of the company profile is that it will provide instant, time-saving factual information. Journalists on a newsroom shift are unlikely to know anything whatsoever about your organisation.

To continue our dairy example, the calls you get initially won't be from a knowledgeable farming correspondent, but a straight-forward 'news' reporter. He or she will need to know as much background as possible to help to meet a deadline.

4. Be prepared to give TV/radio interviews.

PA copy is useful for radio and TV stations, but the chances are that they will wish to put your words back into your mouth for the sake of the broadcast news. They will probably bid for interview facilities. *Only your nominated spokesperson* should give these. Above all, you will need to project a consistent line through the media, and if they've already spoken to 'Old Harry in the works', you could have an additional presentational problem on your hands.

Offer to do radio interviews 'down the line' (ie, on the telephone) for the sake of speed. And when the TV people contact you, they will hopefully have already seen the PA story, thus saving time and avoiding time-consuming briefing at a basic level. Your nominated spokesperson should have phone numbers to hand for local TV and radio stations. Before granting an interview, check if the TV station will be providing material for network (national) news, and if the radio station will be doing likewise (via the BBC or independent radio news). If so, this could avoid your doing several similar interviews for different stations.

5. Offer a daily briefing/update session.

With a big story, perhaps running over a couple of days, your nominated spokesperson should offer a regular updating and briefing session to the media. As a rule, twice a day will be ample. One briefing at, say, 11 am and another at 4 pm will probably satisfy most media outlets. Each can then meet their set deadlines, and each knows that you aren't doing any sneaky 'back-door' stuff with their rivals. For details, see Chapter 8.

In conclusion, you have no choice but to offer full co-operation to the media. If you don't inform, they can misinform.

PR contingency plan checklist

Use this checklist to ensure that you have a PR contingency plan:

1. Have you nominated a spokesperson?
2. Has the spokesperson prepared a briefing sheet for press use?
3. Has the spokesperson done at least one radio/TV interview (in normal, pro-active circumstances)?
4. What is the name and telephone/fax number of the local Press Association correspondent? (Details from Press Association in London, 071-353 7440.)
5. What are the phone/fax numbers of the key local media outlets?
    BBC TV
    Independent TV
    BBC local radio
    ILR (independent local radio)
    Evening newspaper
    Weekly newspaper

Case study

Incident
The M1 air crash, 9 January 1989

Company
British Midland Airways

Background
Recognising that the travel industry is particularly vulnerable to adverse publicity when disaster strikes, Channel 4's *Media Show* interviewed Michael Bishop, Chairman of British Midland Airways, about how he coped with crisis management at Kegworth.

Mr Bishop made two very interesting points:

1. The public (through the media) wants to see somebody senior in charge of whatever has occurred, to reassure them that all that *can* be done *is* being done; and
2. It is an 'old-fashioned' notion to think that the less you say, the less will be reported.

'The early hours immediately after the event are crucial', said Mr

Bishop; 'Little information about the causes will be known, so general background is very useful at this point. The more authoritative the source, the better.'

Larger companies now use specialist PR crisis managers to train switchboard staff. They also ensure that a fully briefed company spokesman is available wherever the media are congregating to report the event.

Useful Addresses

BBC World Service
Bush House
The Strand
London WC2B 4PH
071-257 2039

British Sky Broadcasting
6 Centaurs Business Park
Grant Way
Isleworth
Middlesex TW7 5QD
081-782 3000 (Fax: 081-782 9902)

Department of Trade and Industry
1–19 Victoria Street
London SW1H 0ET
071-215 7877
For regional offices of the DTI, see your local telephone directory.

Market Research Society
15 Northburgh Street
London EC1B 0AH
071-490 4911

Press Association
85 Fleet Street
London EC4P 4BE
071-353 7440

Decent Exposure

Radio Marketing Bureau
46 Westbourne Grove
London W2 5SH
071-221 2535

Bibliography

References

British Rate and Data (BRAD), monthly

Handling Newspaper Text (Editing and Design II), by Harold Evans,
Heinemann, 1974

How to Write Articles for Profit and PR, by Mel Lewis, Kogan Page,
1989

Radio: the Facts, Radio Marketing Bureau, 1988/89

Stalker, by John Stalker, the former Deputy Chief Constable of
the Greater Manchester Police Force, Harrap, 1988

The Writer's Handbook, edited by Barry Turner, Macmillan/PE,
annual

The Writers' and Artists' Yearbook, A & C Black, annual

Willings Press Guide, British Media Publications, annual

Further Reading

The following titles have been published by Kogan Page; a complete list of business books is available from the address on page 4.

Be Your Own PR Man, Michael Bland, 2nd edition, 1987

The Corporate Image: Strategies for Effective Identity Programmes, Nicholas Ind, 1990

How to Increase Sales Without Leaving Your Desk, Edmund Tirbutt, 1991

How to Promote Your Own Business: A Guide to Low Budget Publicity, James Dudley, 1987

Promoting Yourself on TV and Radio, Michael Bland and Simone Mondésir, 1987

The Public Relations Case Book, Alan Capper and Peter Cunard, 1990

Successful Marketing for the Small Business, Dave Patten, 2nd edition, 1988

Index